ACCIDENTS

In North American Climbing 2018

Volume 11 | Number 3 | Issue 71

AMERICAN ALPINE CLUB
GOLDEN, COLORADO

ALPINE CLUB OF CANADA
CANMORE, ALBERTA

CONTENTS

6   Preface

FEATURE ARTICLES

8   Know the Ropes: Safer 4th Class
16   Danger Zones: Mt. Hood

ACCIDENTS & ANALYSIS

22   United States
110 Canada

ESSENTIALS

33   Lower Leg Injuries
83   Evacuate an Injured Patient
113 Avalanche Response

TABLES

120 Annual Data Summary

Front Cover: Ridge climbing in the High Sierra. Photo by Ken Etzel / kenetzelphoto.com.
Back Cover: Colorado Flight for Life in action.

© 2018 The American Alpine Club

ISBN: 978-0-9998556-1-4; (e-book) 978-0-9998556-3-8. Manufactured in the United States. Published by the American Alpine Club, 710 Tenth Street, Suite 100, Golden, CO, 80401, www.americanalpineclub.org.

ACCIDENTS IN NORTH AMERICAN CLIMBING

American Alpine Club

EDITOR EMERITUS
John E. (Jed) Williamson

EDITOR
Dougald MacDonald

SENIOR EDITOR
R. Bryan Simon

CONTRIBUTING EDITORS
Aram Attarian, Joel Peach, Dave Weber

REGIONAL EDITORS
Aram Attarian (Southeast); Lindsay Auble & Lee
Smith (CO); Stacia Glenn (WA); Sarah Koniewicz
(Midwest); Dara Miles (NY & PA); R. Bryan Simon
(WV); Eric Ratkowski (Shawangunks, NY); Nikki
Smith (UT); Michael Wejchert (NH)

DESIGN
David Boersma

ADDITIONAL THANKS
Ken Etzel, Ron Funderburke, Ian Jackson,
Liberty Mountain, Julie Moyer, Leo Paik, Tim
Ozerkov, Jim Pasterczyk, Petzl, John Reilly

Alpine Club of Canada

SAFETY COMMITTEE
Hai Pham
safety@alpineclubofcanada.ca

CANADIAN CONTENT EDITOR
Robert Chisnall
anam@alpineclubofcanada.ca

PREFACE

By Dougald MacDonald

I would be very happy if every reader of this book would make a simple three-step pledge. Doing so might save a few lives. A few of your own lives.

This year's edition reports a worrying leap in the number of accidents while lowering or preparing to lower from anchors atop single-pitch climbs. Having seen growing numbers of such accidents in recent years, we introduced lowering errors as a primary accident cause in our data tables in the 2016 edition; the errors include too-short ropes slipping through a belayer's device, communication mix-ups, and failure to retie properly at an anchor. In 2016, we recorded five such incidents. The following year, we counted six. *This year we documented 12 lowering accidents.*

Now this could be just a statistical blip. I sure hope so. It also might reflect the much-discussed "gym to crag" phenomenon, in which ill-prepared gym climbers venture outside without adequate mentoring. But here's the thing: About half of the climbers and belayers in this year's lowering reports were highly experienced. And yet they still made simple, extremely dangerous mistakes.

So, let's all pledge to take three basic steps on every single-pitch climb:

1. **Make a plan and communicate the plan**. Before each climb, tell your belayer if you plan to lower or rappel from the anchor, and stick to that plan. If circumstances force a change—like forgetting your rappel device—be absolutely certain your belayer understands the new plan before you weight the rope.

2. **Tie a stopper knot in the belayer's end of the rope**. Or tie in the belayer. Absolutely no exceptions.

3. **Weight-test your system before unclipping from the anchor**. Whether rappelling or lowering, find a way to test the ropes before committing to them.

These steps won't prevent every single lowering or communication error. But if everyone involved in lowering accidents in 2017 had followed all three steps, up to a dozen fewer climbers would have been injured or killed. Make the pledge. And insist that your climbing partners do too.

CONTRIBUTE

Submissions

Visit *publications.americanalpineclub.org/accidents_submission* to file a report online. Or email us at *accidents@americanalpineclub.org*.

Friends of Accidents

The following people and organizations recently have donated $100 or more specifically to support *Accidents in North American Climbing*. Thank you! Make your own contribution at *americanalpineclub.org/donate*.

Laura Chedalawada	Yannick Gingras	Jim Small
Charles Eiriksson Jr.	Eric Green	Douglas Wilson
Carla Firey	Dougald MacDonald	
Lee Freitag	Scott Petersen	

THE SHARP END

Join the more than 30,000 people who listen to the Sharp End podcast each month. Hosted by Ashley Saupe, the Sharp End features interviews with climbers, rangers, and rescue professionals, based on the stories in *Accidents in North American Climbing*.

The Sharp End is sponsored for 2018 by Mammut, with additional support from Colorado Outward Bound School, Suunto, and other companies. Find it wherever you listen to podcasts.

AAC RESCUE BENEFITS

Membership in the American Alpine Club qualifies you for rescue benefits in case things go wrong during any human-powered, land-based activity beyond the trailhead. With up to $12,500 available, we've got you covered.

Trailhead Rescue
- $7,500 in global coverage, including the United States
- No elevation restriction
- Member discount on expanded coverage
- 31 AAC members were rescued in 2017 thanks to the Trailhead Rescue Benefit
- To use the Trailhead Rescue Benefit, members must call Global Rescue at (617) 459-4200 as soon as possible during an emergency

Domestic Rescue
- Up to $5,000 in in reimbursement for out-of-pocket rescue expenses within the U.S. only. Canada and Mexico are excluded.
- File a claim within 60 days of rescue by emailing claims@americanalpineclub.org or by calling (303) 384-0110
- Medical and ambulance expenses do not qualify
- Reimbursement subject to verification and approval

Activities Covered
Climbing, hiking, backcountry skiing, mountain biking, and more. If it's human-powered, on land, and you're rescued, you're covered as long as you're an active AAC member. Note: Basic coverage does not include search, ambulance services, or medical care.

Upgrades
Planning to climb internationally? We recommend upgrading to a full Global Rescue membership with a 5 percent AAC discount. Upgrades include field rescue, medical consultation, and evacuation. Learn more at *americanalpineclub.org/rescue* or call 1-800-381-9571.

Five climbers died on Capitol Peak in Colorado in 2017 (see p.. 65). Though few rope up for this peak, simple rope techniques could increase climbers' confidence, keep them on route, and prevent falls. *Katie Botwin*

Know the Ropes

SAFER 4TH CLASS

Managing risk on easier terrain

BY TICO GANGULEE

Managing terrain with a low probability but high consequence of falling–typically described as third-class, fourth-class, and low fifth-class climbing–is a multi-faceted affair, affected by skill sets, route and time pressures, and human factors (the psychological factors, sometimes called heuristic traps, that can impact judgment). Tumbling down a 30-foot, low-angle gully or "approach pitch" may not appear as terrifying as falling off an overhang while roped, but it's usually far more dangerous.

Each year we see many accidents that very likely could have been prevented or mitigated by the use of a rope in easy terrain, including unroped falls on technical alpine ridges (often caused by loose rock), approach and descent accidents due to rockfall or small slips, and scrambling accidents in terrain deemed "too easy for a rope." This article seeks to make climbers aware of alternatives to soloing (scrambling) that use the equipment they're likely carrying anyway and incur little or no time cost.

The terrain that best utilizes these techniques is likely too easy for fully pitching out yet will occasionally be the scene of a preventable accident—the prevention being the appropriate use of a rope. Examples include the Cables Route on the north face of Longs Peak, much of the north ridge of Mt. Conness, descending the summit pyramid on Mt. Shuksan, or even going over Asterisk Pass at Smith Rock. While many people are loathe to break out the rope for easy climbing, the added security and confidence often allow climbers to move faster, actually speeding up the climb.

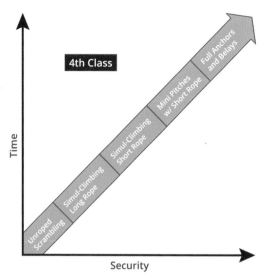

All terrain, regardless of the severity, should be managed in one way or another. With pace, attentiveness, and equipment selection, we even manage class 1 terrain such as a trail. The best management of any terrain is the style that minimizes the probability and consequence of a fall, while keeping in mind the need for efficiency. Strive for consistent, rational judgments of terrain severity. Could you travel easily with an open cup of coffee? If not, consider adding safety systems. What's the consequence of a slip or stumble? If it's injury or death, consider adding safety systems. We practice and train climbing movement to get better—we also should practice and train using the rope on easier terrain.

PLANNING AND MOVEMENT

While this article covers methodologies with the rope, it's important to remember that movement ability is a prime risk-management strategy for mountain travel, and there are many ways to set yourself up for success. If you never fall, the rope tricks you learn are just a fun but academic exercise. Here are some strategies for preventing falls that don't involve a rope:

- *Plan ahead.* Research the approach and descent as thoroughly as the climb. Don't gloss over descriptions of the "easy" stretches of a route—study them as well as the cruxes. If time allows, scout the approach or descent the afternoon before the climb.
- *Choose appropriate footwear.* While flipflops can work for cragging approaches or descents, a sticky-rubber approach shoe or running shoe provides much more security.
- *Wear your harness and helmet all day.* Don't wait until you're perched on a precarious ledge to gear up. And keep your harness on during the descent—you'll be more likely to use the rope appropriately.
- *Be vigilant for loose rock.* Test all handholds, footholds, and blocks before

committing to them. Climb and scramble gingerly.

- *Rest and eat.* Having a quick snack before a long descent not only improves mental clarity, it also can offer time to scope the descent and communicate a plan to partners.

ROPING UP WITHOUT ANCHORS

Try to set your nonsense filter fairly high when using the rope: If you're roped without enough solid anchors somewhere in the system to stop a fall, the rope may be creating more potential harm than good.

"Confidence roping" is a concept used by a small cadre of hiking guides, mainly in Europe. It involves using a rope to ease the mind but not protect the body. Recreationally, this technique is not at all appropriate, as it is not designed to actually stop a fall or prevent injury.

Many guides employ "short-roping" to provide security for their guest in terrain where the consequences of a fall would be injurious or fatal, but not so steep to warrant pitching out (due to time pressure). Short-roping is not, as the media sometimes depicts, a small, brown man relentlessly dragging his exhausted white client to a Himalayan summit. It is a technique where a skilled, attentive guide can stop unwanted acceleration from becoming unmanageable—that is, preventing a slip from progressing to a fall.

Short-roping allows the team to move together as fast or faster than the weakest party member would move while soloing. However, it relies heavily on the guide's movement and rope-handling skills, and most importantly the nature of the terrain: Ledgy, blocky 4th class might be very manageable, but a 60° slick slab or ice might not. Because of the reliance on specific movement skills, short-roping is seldom appropriate for the recreational climber. It's often overused even by trained professional guides.

Simul-climb tactics: The leader, belayed off the ground, placed a low piece to protect a hard move. Before the second makes the same move, the leader passes his rope around a horn for security. *Ron Funderburke*

Rather than relying on the rope alone, most recreational climbers should focus on techniques that combine the rope and terrain or placed protection. If no anchors or terrain features between climbers can be found, it may be safer for the team to solo than to stay roped up. Relying on the rope without any protection is a relatively unusual circumstance for the experienced climber, and if you are encountering it often there may be another deficit in your skill set to address, be it technical or ideological.

SIMUL-CLIMBING

While it has its pitfalls, simul-climbing is heavily used by experienced parties in easier terrain, including approaches and descents. Simul-climbing is when two or three party members climb at the same time, linked by the rope, with security provided by the leader placing gear so there is always protection between each climber. (Terrain features can be used in a similar way.) Pacing and communication between the climbers prevent excess slack from developing.

An important part of the technique lies in using the correct length of rope between climbers. Longer lengths of rope may allow for steeper steps to be climbed without both climbers in steep terrain at the same time, but they also can dredge gullies and dislodge rocks, creating a hazard. Longer lengths of rope also are suboptimal for communication—most simulclimbers will want to chat about what they need along the way ("Can you move faster for a second?" "Could you stop there?"). Remember, the point is to limit the length of a fall, and if you're traveling with 150 feet of rope between partners and very little gear, you may be putting the leader at risk for a very long fall.

On the other hand, too short a rope length can be annoying if there are different paces in the team due to ability or terrain. And it can become dangerous if a climber becomes "trapped" on difficult terrain when the rope stops moving or pulls too hard in either direction.

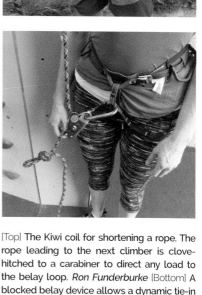

[Top] The Kiwi coil for shortening a rope. The rope leading to the next climber is clove-hitched to a carabiner to direct any load to the belay loop. *Ron Funderburke* [Bottom] A blocked belay device allows a dynamic tie-in while simul-climbing. *Tico Gangulee*

It's a good practice to slightly overestimate the necessary length of rope, then take in coils as soon as you notice you're starting to hold coils of rope or loops are dragging. A good place to start is 50 feet or so between climbers, then reassess and dial in the length. Using a Grigri blocked by a knot or plate device in guide mode can offer a dynamic tie-in and easy rope adjustment, but in simpler terrain this often just adds unnecessary complexity. When shortening the rope for simuling, the extra rope can be carried either in a Kiwi coil or in the pack, with each climber tying off or clipping into the harness.

How much gear to place between climbers is very dependent on the terrain, conditions, and ability of the climbers: 5.10 leaders on dry 5.2 might motor along with two or three cams between them, but may want more in verglassed 4th class (especially in rock shoes). Camming devices are often faster to place and remove than nuts. The leader should use as much of the rack as possible before transitioning, as long as he or she has adequate materials for

Two climbers seconding on either side of a ridge so that neither will take a long pendulum fall. The same principle applies while simul-climbing. *Vetta Mountain Guides*

an anchor at the end of the "pitch." For a quick belay anchor when transitioning to a short belayed pitch, wrapping the rope a couple times around a horn or using a Connecticut tree hitch (an easily released hitch blocked by a carabiner) on a thigh-diameter or bigger tree can be entirely adequate.

Using terrain features when simul-climbing can provide "free" protection (i.e., protection with no time cost or gear cost). This is primarily accomplished by routing the rope over features, like rock horns or strong trees, that would stop a tumble. Having partners move on either side of a rock or snow ridge (relatively close to each other, as communication can become a factor) can provide a great deal of free security, as long as the terrain isn't significantly more difficult on one side versus the other.

Transitions in simul-climbing—from simuling to belaying or vice versa—are where the magic happens for the skilled and the process falls apart for the unpracticed. It's important to be able to quickly provide a belay to the second from a stance. Consider the hierarchy of belay techniques, and then apply the most appropriate: hand belay, hip/shoulder belay, or belay off a plate or Munter hitch. Transitions are also a good time to get on the same page with your partner about route finding, pacing, etc.

Generally, the stronger climber should go second, as counterintuitive as this seems; the consequences of the second falling and pulling the leader down are greater than the leader falling. (However, if one member knows the route better, it may be prudent for that climber to be in the lead.) Off-label use of progress-capture devices like the Petzl Micro Traxion or Tibloc, clipped to solid intermediate protection points, can mitigate the danger caused by a second's fall, but their use is more appropriate in difficult terrain than for traditional simul-climbing ground.

A team of three adds potential load to the system and requires additional terrain judgement and more conservative strategies when difficulties arise. (This is one of the risks that can be managed in planning for an objective, by adding or subtracting team members.) Considerations include whether to space the climbers evenly or have the bottom two close together, and whether the second climber, when spaced evenly, should clean the protection or re-clip it for the third. These considerations are impacted by terrain and ability.

As with two climbers, a longer distance between the lower team members in a team of three can mitigate some of the pacing problems when transitioning from easier to harder climbing, but adding rope to the system can create other problems. One option is to attach the middle climber to the rope using a Micro Traxion or other live-load-rated progress-capture device, either directly or with a short tether. In the case of a fall, the progress-capture device will grab the rope. This technique allows the climber to move at any pace, including moving back down the rope. This method requires high confidence in rock quality, availability and quality of protection, and movement skills, but it can allow for three people to move through fourth-class terrain very quickly. It loses appropriateness as difficulty rises.

A quick terrain belay around a solid horn protects a stretch of easy but exposed ground. Ideally, this horn would be less rounded on the brake-hand side to offer more control. *Vetta Mountain Guides*

SHORT PITCHING

Very short belayed sections can quickly add security to long stretches of scrambling or simul-climbing. Consider using this technique for terrain that seems to be harder than expected or when there's any doubt about route-finding. Don't just "climb and hope."

Quickly switching to belayed climbing requires practice and, more importantly, vision. Being able to see terrain well ahead of you, note when you would likely want a belay, and identify a simple belay anchor are skills learned through practice (and mentoring, if available).

Often, a series of short pitches using "terrain belays" can be a fast yet secure way through ground that is complex or unfamiliar. A terrain belay uses the friction of the rope around a rock to provide security—it's like a hip belay but wrapping the rope around an immovable rock horn or boulder instead of your body. Speed and efficiency are gained by not having to build anchors.

The keys to using a terrain belay effectively are identifying a horn or boulder that's big and well-anchored enough that there is no chance it will move under load. Give the rock a good shake and then place one hand on the horn and hit it with the other hand—you want to feel little to no vibration. Be sure the shape of the horn and anticipated direction of load mean the rope has zero chance of slipping off.

In order to limit rope abrasion, don't drag the rope over the horn as much as lift it and place it as you're belaying. (The movement is very similar to belaying off a plate device in guide mode.) A refinement for using features too tall to place the rope over is to simply pass a bight of rope around the feature and belay using the side of the bight that goes to the following climber; there's no need to untie, and this provides a modicum of security to the belayer as well.

A thigh-diameter or larger tree, when well rooted, makes a good belay point, but terrain belays on trees can put a lot of sap on the rope and damage the tree. A basket- or girth-hitched sling around the tree and a belay off a Munter hitch will be nearly as fast.

Short pitching requires placing protection at reasonable intervals—soloing 50-foot pitches isn't any safer than just plain soloing. In loose terrain, it's vital to protect the whole pitch, not just the hardest moves, so place a piece every few body lengths or whenever you pause to scope the route ahead. Cams are often faster than nuts to place and clean. Favor larger or simpler protection (larger cams, slung horns or trees, routing across a ridge) and avoid smaller or more finicky gear, unless it is the only option. Keep in mind the big picture: managing the consequence of an unexpected fall.

DESCENDING 3RD AND 4TH CLASS

Probably the most appropriate yet underutilized time to belay on easy terrain is when descending, especially when descending an unknown technical route. Having someone down-lead a short pitch from an anchor provides more options than rappelling, as it's easier to reverse a short downclimb than to reverse a rappel.

When down-leading, placing protection for the second is of vital importance. Place solid gear directly after (below) any difficult or insecure moves, as the second will be effectively "leading" this part. Remember to place gear high enough that a ledge fall would be mitigated, which often means placing gear early in the downclimb.

Simul-climbing is also useful during descents. Downclimbing hundreds of feet of fourth class, as many alpine routes require, can be difficult and dangerous at the end of a long day, and adding a rope with protection between the climbers not only may be safer but also can help keep a team together, communicating, and focused.

Down-leading a short pitch: The climber places a piece below a tricky step to protect the second person's downclimb. Note the use of friction over a smooth ridge for a terrain belay. *Ron Funderburke*

Rappelling low-angle terrain can be both tedious and dangerous; the ropes can easily turn into a cluster, and pulling the rope through loose rock is hazardous. Traditional methods like carrying the ends of the rope in saddlebags or stacking the extra rope in the pack are effective, but often time-consuming. The J-rig rope throw can help get the rope down as well.

The J-rig starts as a regular rappel, but without throwing or lowering the rope ends; instead the second feeds the rope to the first rappeler until the second is holding the ends at the upper anchor. He or she then throws the ends out and over the first rappeler.

A variation to the J-rig rappel: The first rappeller keeps the ends of the ropes with him to prevent them from snagging below. *Ron Funderburke*

When rappelling short steps, the equivocation hitch (a.k.a. death daisy or death macrame) can mitigate many issues, including having to pull the entire rope across a rock horn or tree anchor. With this hitch, climbers can lower or rappel on one strand, then pull the other strand to retrieve the rope. The equivocation hitch can be tied without having the ends of the rope available, so there's no need for climbers to untie before rappelling. This technique is best for advanced climbers and is beyond the scope of this article to teach. *The Mountain Guide Manual* (Chauvin and Coppolillo, 2017) provides an excellent explanation and photos.

When transitioning from rappel to downclimbing, it's often possible and prudent to use the existing rappel anchor as a belay anchor if the terrain warrants and there's rope available. Say the required rappel is only 50 feet–after rappelling with a doubled 200-foot rope, another 100 feet of rope could be made available for a belayed downclimb before pulling the rope. Once both climbers have rappelled, one climber can clip or tie into one rope end and clove hitch into the other strand, creating a closed loop to the anchor above. The other climber then can downclimb while belayed by the person above, placing gear along the way to protect the second one down. Be aware of rockfall hazard when pulling the rope after separating the party members. Separating the climbers also makes a stuck rappel rope potentially more time-consuming to deal with if it requires leading back up.

CONCLUSION

It's essential to realize that the techniques described in this article are meant to be insurance against the totally unexpected. If a fall is considered to be in the realm of possibility, you should not be simul-climbing or otherwise running it out. Just belay and protect pitches as usual (or leave gear and rappel when descending). We don't think, "Well, I've got a seatbelt on, I might as well drive drunk." We shouldn't just think, "Well, I've got a rope on, I'll be fine even if the terrain is harder than I expected."

Tico Gangulee (@darkstarmtguide) is an IFMGA guide and AIARE avalanche educator, living with his wife and son in the alpine mecca of Houston. He works internationally and in southwestern Colorado. The author thanks Marc Chauvin, co-author of the Mountain Guide Manual, for developing or promoting several concepts covered in this article.

Mt. Hood's mystique draws many thousands to attempt the mountain each year. *Timothy Ozerkov*

Danger Zones
MT. HOOD
BY JOEL PEACH

Though the exact number is unknown, the U.S. Forest Service estimates that at least 10,000 people attempt to climb Mt. Hood annually. Just an hour and a half from the Portland area's 2.4 million residents and easily visible from downtown, Mt. Hood has an alluring mystique. You can drive to 6,000 feet, and the 11,249-foot summit looks close and easy to reach.

But as the Forest Service warns on its Mt. Hood webpage, "There are no hiking trails to the summit." And like any large, glaciated mountain, Hood presents objective mountaineering risks. As a result, many Mt. Hood accidents and rescues have been described in the pages of *Accidents in North American Climbing*.

We searched the last 40 years of our database to identify accidents and near misses on Mt. Hood and pinpoint their causes. We also consulted with guides and search and rescue volunteers on the mountain. While the record contained in *Accidents* is far from complete (not all accidents that occur are reported, and not all reported accidents are included in the book), our survey is a representative sample of the situations climbers are likely to encounter on Mt. Hood and on similar peaks with easy to moderately difficult snow and ice climbs.

Well over half the incidents on Mt. Hood took place on the popular South Side route (a.k.a. Palmer Glacier or Hogsback route) and its variations. Most of these accidents were above the Hogsback and the bergschrund, particularly in or near the chutes that penetrate the rime-covered rocks below the summit. The South Side is also the most common descent route from Hood's summit, and about three-quarters of all South Side accidents happened on the way down. The Leuthold Couloir, above the Reid Glacier on the west side of Mt. Hood, and the Cooper Spur on the northeast also saw higher concentrations of incidents than other routes.

Though there are accidents on Mt. Hood throughout the year, half of the ones in our data were in May or June, which are two of the most popular months to attempt the mountain. Hood's peak season is late winter through late spring, when most crevasses are filled or well bridged and rockfall danger is significantly less than later in summer.

What follows is our analysis of incidents in the archives and recommendations for safer travel on Mt. Hood and similar environments.

FALLS ON SNOW AND ICE

By a significant margin, most accidents on Mt. Hood involved climbers falling on snow or ice. Many parties were not properly equipped for travel on such terrain. Among those that were, a number did not possess the skill to use their equipment or had it "safely" stowed away in a pack where it could not help them.

Injuries occurred not only during actual falls, but also when climbers slid into rocks, crevasses, or fumaroles, the crevasse-like holes opened in Hood's upper snow slopes by hot volcanic gases (*see more on fumaroles below*).

SELF-ARREST

Climbers on Mt. Hood, particularly those climbing solo or unroped, should be skilled in self-arrest techniques and climb in conditions where a self-arrest is likely to work. The inability to stop can mean a slide of hundreds of feet.

Our reports make it clear that ski poles and hiking sticks are no substitute for a mountaineering ice axe, even on Mt. Hood's easiest route. After one 300-foot fall, in June 2012, an injured climber was asked why he carried a trekking pole instead of an axe. "I travel light" was the response.

Sometimes, even with correct equipment and technique, self-arrest is not possible due to surface snow conditions. An incident in January 1994 illustrated this when a climber resting by Crater Rock on the South Side slipped on ice that had formed after warm days and cold winter nights. One of his climbing partners attempted to grab him and then fell himself. Neither was able to self-arrest on the icy surface, and the two slid more than 1,000 feet.

It's important to know when climbing conditions are unfavorable for self-arrest and alternative risk mitigation (such as belayed, protected climbing) may be prudent. The Northwest Avalanche Center and the U.S. Forest Service's Mt. Hood office and webpage are good sources of conditions information.

CRAMPONS

Loose or ill-fitting crampons have caused a number of accidents. Proper mountaineering boots should be worn, and the crampons must be fitted to the specific boots before one's ascent. Ensure that crampons with bails are used only with boots that have sufficient heel or toe welts to hold the bails securely.

Crampon points should be kept sharp. In March 2001, a climber slipped while descending the Pearly Gates chute on the South Side and fell hundreds of feet down the Hogsback. The climber's crampons had been rented from an outdoor shop and were found to have extremely dull points, likely contributing to the fall.

Care must be taken to mitigate the impact of warm snow balling up underneath crampons, making them more prone to slipping. In three accidents (one fatal), balled-up crampons were suspected in climber falls. "Anti-bot" snow plates on crampons help a lot, and climbers should take care to knock snow off their crampons frequently, especially during descents. If the snow can't be adequately cleared from crampons, consider adding a belay to protect against falls.

More than one injurious fall resulted from a climber catching a crampon point on hard snow, clothing, or other gear while walking. Great care must be taken when jumping over crevasses or other slots. In June 1989, two climbers in the same party suffered knee and leg injuries in jumps over the bergschrund (then only two feet wide) while descending the South Side. A more controlled climb (belayed, if needed) or end run around a crevasse is recommended over jumping.

GLISSADING

Though glissading can be a quick and fun way to descend moderate snow slopes, out-of-control or poorly planned glissades have led to several accidents on Mt. Hood. In a 1993 report, a novice climber with no ice axe glissaded over a large cliff below the Hogsback and tumbled a few hundred feet. In 1994, in the same general area, another climber lost control of a glissade and took a 700-foot slide onto the upper White River Glacier. Glissades should not be attempted unless the climber is equipped with an axe and knows how to self-arrest, the snow surface is not too icy, and the full glissade route is visible and free of obstacles.

On Hood and other snowy peaks, accidents caused by glissading with crampons are common, as crampon points frequently snag hard snow or ice, causing lower-leg injuries and/or tumbling falls. An editor's note in our publication after one such incident in 1997 quoted longtime guide George Hurley: "There is no good reason for glissading with sharp spikes on our feet."

ROPED TRAVEL

Although roping up on steep snow might seem like a good way to prevent some of the accidents described above, Hood's South Side is commonly climbed unroped. More importantly, our incident reports demonstrate some flawed risk assessment and technique when roping up.

Pete Keane, director of Timberline Mountain Guides, one of two guide services authorized to operate on Mt. Hood, points out that many climbers apply the thinking and rope techniques suitable for glaciated climbs on the South Side route, which has few crevasses or crevasse-like hazards. "People are confusing falling *into* the mountain with falling *off* the mountain as the primary hazard," Keane says.

Accidents involving roped parties may involve climbers ascending or descending without belays or protection, making it quite possible for one sliding climber to pull off his or her teammates. In an incident in 2002, three roped teams of 10 climbers were pulled from the mountain when climbers in the highest roped team fell. The four members of the upper team were each separated by about 35 feet, and when they were unable to arrest, they clotheslined the teams below. Four climbers were critically injured and three were killed.

Roped travel without a belay may be necessary to guard against crevasse falls on Hood's more glaciated routes. But when climbers choose to rope up for the steeper terrain on the South Side, they should have a plan for creating running protection (usually pickets) and/or belays.

DANGER FROM ABOVE

Conical stratovolcanoes like Hood are composed of built-up lava, pumice, and ash, which

Crowds are common in the summit chutes. Belay anchors or running protection can keep a roped party from "clotheslining" others in case of a fall. *Timothy Ozerkov*

means there are lots of loose rocks ready to fall down the mountain when seasonal or daily warming cycles melt the ice and rime anchoring the rocks. Falling ice is also a hazard, especially as winter loosens its grip on the mountain.

A number of our accident reports involved climbers struck by falling debris, directly causing injury or precipitating injurious or fatal falls. In other cases, rotten rock gave way underfoot. In 2004, for example, a late-season climber on the Hogsback dislodged a rock and fell onto an ice slope, sliding 200 feet and fracturing his leg.

AVALANCHE

Mt. Hood gets climbed (and skied) nearly year-round, and with heavy snowfall on the mountain, avalanches are a threat throughout the winter and spring. All three of the avalanche incidents documented in our pages were in spring or early summer: two in late May and one in late June, including two slides above the Reid Glacier in the same year.

In one case, heavy snow was saturated with rain that froze and then rapidly warmed on a hot, sunny day. In another, on West Crater Rim, a storm loaded fresh snow over an old crust, and rapid warming then released a slide that swept off climbers.

The third avalanche, above the Reid Glacier, was interesting in that the climbers weren't directly swept away by the snow. Instead, their rope was caught, pulling them off. As mentioned above, climbers should weigh the risks of falling versus other hazards when deciding whether to rope up; in some cases the speed of unroped climbing may expose one to less risk from avalanche, rockfall, and icefall.

Climbers should learn snow evaluation skills and inquire about avalanche conditions before heading out. (In the case of the West Crater Rim avalanche, a sign had been posted at the climbers' register at Timberline Lodge that read, "High Avalanche Hazard.") Avalanche transceivers for all members in a party are recommended in early season or anytime avalanche hazard is rated considerable or higher.

Though the Northwest Avalanche Center's regular forecasts (www.nwac.us) are limited to winter and spring, the center provides general summertime guidance and avalanche courses to help climbers evaluate snow conditions.

WEATHER AND NAVIGATION

In May 1986, despite poor weather and a bad forecast, a party of 20 headed up the South Side route. As the weather worsened, several members of the party turned back. By the time the trip leader convinced the rest of the group to retreat, winds were approaching 45 mph. In visibility below 10 feet, and after making a compass error, the remaining group built a snow cave in an effort to sit through the storm. With only a single shovel (which was eventually lost), the cave they dug couldn't accommodate the entire group, and they rotated inside throughout the night. The rescue took two days, and nine of the climbers died from exposure.

Christopher Van Tilburg, a doctor and longtime member of the Crag Rats rescue team on Mt. Hood's north side, observed that, "Hood is a monolith above a forest at 4,000 to 6,000 feet, with no other mountains around and in a maritime climate." Such tall, isolated peaks obstruct moist airflow, creating standing atmospheric waves that result in rapid formation of lenticular clouds and precipitation. The weather patterns here are different than those found in the Rockies and other U.S. ranges, so visiting climbers may not be aware of warning signs for foul weather.

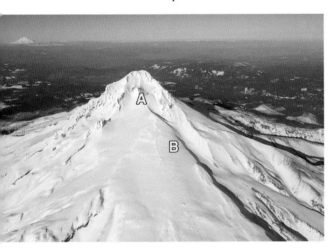

The "Mt. Hood Triangle" is obvious from the air on the mountain's south aspect. Heading straight down the fall line from Crater Rock (A) leads climbers away from the proper descent route (B). Follow a magnetic south (180°) compass bearing from Crater Rock to stay on track. *Timothy Ozerkov*

It almost goes without saying that climbers should study the weather forecast, but conditions on Hood can change unexpectedly and rapidly. Climbers should not continue upward into a storm or low visibility, hoping the weather may improve. All climbers should pack appropriate clothing for changing weather and the possibility of having to bivy on the mountain.

NAVIGATION ON DESCENT

One consequence of poor weather is the increased challenge of navigating the South Side descent. In poor visibility, especially in a whiteout, climbers who simply head downhill along the fall line will angle to skier's right, away from the ascent route and Timberline Lodge, and toward the cliffs and canyons farther west. Traversing too far to the east between Crater Rock and Devil's Kitchen can lead people off-route into the White River Glacier.

In poor visibility, climbers should pause on the east side of Crater Rock, take a compass bearing of magnetic south (180°), and then follow this bearing across the slopes to reach the east side of the Palmer ski lift and the normal descent alongside the ski slopes. Portland Mountain Rescue has published a PDF (available online) with a diagram of this area (known as the "Mt. Hood Triangle"), along with instructions and GPS coordinates for the South Side descent. Similar information is available at the Forest Service's Mt. Hood climbing page.

OTHER ISSUES

One of the oldest incident reports in our data set (1976) features a case of pulmonary edema suffered at 8,900 feet by a student in a climbing class. Though Mt. Hood is toward the bottom end of elevations where acute mountain sickness generally occurs, altitude illnesses are not unknown on Hood. Altitude-related symptoms may contribute to poor decision-making or stumbling.

Climbers should familiarize themselves with the signs and symptoms of altitude illness. If acute mountain sickness develops, descent is the best remedy.

FUMAROLES

A unique hazard on Mt. Hood is crevasse-like fumaroles, especially the one in the Hot Rocks area, located in the run-out below the Old Chute (Mazama Chute). Not only is there risk of falling into the fumarole because of weakened snow bridges (skirt the area widely) or an uncontrolled slide, entering a fumarole also is dangerous because of poisonous gases. These gases pool at the bottom of the hole, potentially adding hypoxia to the list of a fall victim's problems.

CROWDING

Mt. Hood's popularity can mean lines of climbers starting up the crux chutes of the South Side or waiting to descend. Patience is a virtue—rushing risks entanglement with other parties, as well as increased risk of knocking rock or ice onto other climbers. Even climbers who might not usually need a rope on Mt. Hood may consider belaying through these terrain traps when crowds threaten.

Rescuing a climber from 100 feet down in a fumarole on Mt. Hood's South Side. *Scott Norton*

The volume of climber traffic and the availability of personal locator beacons and cell phones also increase the likelihood that climbers on popular routes will be able to summon help in an emergency. But don't become one of our statistics. Prepare well for a Mt. Hood climb with the skills and equipment required for such a peak—a mountain that may seem easy but can quickly become dangerous.

Joel Peach is a contributing editor of Accidents in North American Climbing. Thanks to Pearce Beissinger, Pete Keane, Tim Ozerkov, Jeff Scheetz, and Christopher Van Tilburg for their help with this article. The online version of this story has links to all articles and information sources mentioned here.

Roped for safety while traveling along the Kahiltna Glacier, near the 7,800-foot camp on Denali's West Buttress Route. *Shane Treat, NPS Volunteer Rescuer*

ALASKA

CREVASSE FALL | Climbing Unroped
Denali, West Buttress

At 2:40 p.m. on May 26, Alpine Ascents International (AAI) guide Stuart Robertson reported that a climber on an independent team had fallen into a crevasse while traveling unroped at 8,300 feet on Denali's West Buttress Route. Robertson and fellow AAI guide Michael Hutchins extracted the verbally responsive climber from about 20 meters below the glacier surface while NPS personnel organized evacuation plans. The guides had the patient out of the crevasse at 3:02 p.m. Following an assessment of the 45-year-old male climber by Hutchins, further NPS assistance was requested. As the patient's mental status returned to normal, his chief complaint was severe flank pain; the guides also were concerned about hypothermia. The patient was monitored in a tent until NPS personnel arrived on scene.

Rangers determined that the potential for a lower back injury meant the most appropriate means of transport would be to wait for clear weather to fly the patient to Talkeetna in a vacuum mattress and cervical collar for full spinal-motion restriction. Mountaineering ranger Mik Shain and two NPS volunteers monitored the patient through the night. The following morning, helicopter pilot Andreas Hermansky, with NPS volunteer Jeff Lane as an attendant, flew the patient to Talkeetna, where he transferred to an ambulance at 11:12 a.m.

ANALYSIS
All five of the climbers in this team were on skis but not roped together. Although skis or snowshoes add a margin of safety, rangers discourage unroped or solo travel on Denali's glaciers. Whether roped or unroped, every member of the team must be prepared with both the skills and the equipment to rescue their companions. These climbers had to rely on the good will and fortunate timing of other climbers in the vicinity to rescue their partner. (*Source: Denali Mountaineering Rangers.*)

FROSTBITE
Denali, West Buttress

On May 27, a 53-year-old male, climbing solo, sustained frostbite injuries to all ten of his fingers while ascending from the 14,200-foot camp toward the 17,200-foot camp on the West Buttress. At 9:10 a.m., he made a satelite phone call requesting a rescue. Poor satellite connection prevented any further information from being relayed until 1:45 p.m., when an FRS radio call reached mountaineering ranger Dan Corn at 14,200-foot camp. A climbing party reported passing a non-ambulatory climber with frostbitten fingers lying in a sleeping bag at 16,800 feet.

While the NPS patrol began ascending toward the injured patient's location, Corn learned that climbers Jay Claus and Hans Seeger had begun to lower the patient from Washburn's Thumb, a prominent rock formation along the upper West Buttress. Mountain guides Travis Baldwin, Michael Gardner, and Sebastian Grau assisted with the lowering operation until they rendezvoused with the NPS team at 14,800 feet. The patient was evacuated to 14,200-foot camp, where he was further assessed and received treatment for frostbite in the NPS medical tent.

While waiting for the weather to clear for a helicopter evacuation, Corn and Erickson consulted with frostbite experts at the University of Utah, who recommended prompt thrombolytic therapy (medication for eliminating blood clots). At 8:30 p.m., the patient was flown from 14,200-foot camp directly to the airport in Palmer and transferred to the regional hospital by ambulance.

ANALYSIS

To prevent frostbite, adequate clothing for the prevailing conditions must be worn, and clothing layers that get wet (especially gloves and socks) should be changed for dry layers as soon as practical. It is paramount to actively rewarm any body part(s) that becomes cold and numb, not only to prevent more serious injury but also to accurately assess the severity of injuries. Cold extremities should be rewarmed through skin-to-skin contact; in arctic conditions, frostbit areas likely will not rewarm with exercise alone. (Once rewarmed, frostbitten tissue must not be allowed to refreeze, as this will increase the severity of injury.) When circumstances prevent the rewarming of cooled body parts, climbers must seek shelter or descend to a more hospitable location to prevent the worsening of the injury. (*Source: Denali Mountaineering Rangers.*)

ADDITIONAL FROSTBITE INCIDENTS: *Two more frostbite incidents, involving three patients, required helicopter evacuations from the 14,200-foot camp during the 2017 season. On June 12, a 26-year-old male requested assistance at the medical tent after bivouacking on Denali's summit the night before and suffering deep frostbite injuries to multiple fingers and toes. The climber was treated for frostbite and significant dehydration before being flown out on June 13. Two days later, two climbers from the same team (male, 23 and 27) descended to 14,200-foot camp following a summit attempt the day prior, during which they had frostbit their hands while traversing below Denali Pass. The 23-year-old patient was also exhibiting signs and symptoms indicative of snow blindness. Both climbers were treated overnight and evacuated the next morning via the NPS helicopter. (Source: Denali Mountaineering Rangers.)*

APPENDICITIS
Denali, West Buttress

On June 4, mountaineering ranger Dan Corn and his team assessed a 23-year-old male for stomach pain at the 14,200-foot camp. The climber and Corn decided that self-evacuation to base camp was the best course of action, given his current symptoms.

Later in the day and lower on the mountain, Corn checked in with the climber and found his condition had deteriorated. At 6,700 feet on the Kahiltna Glacier, Corn and his team did another assessment and concluded that appendicitis symptomology seemed likely. The patient was transported to the 7,200-foot base camp via toboggan due to his increased pain and difficulty walking. There, he was treated with pain medication and antibiotics at the NPS medical tent until he could be evacuated by air after sunrise the following morning.

ANALYSIS

Diagnosing a medical illness in the field can prove difficult. The best approach is a complete patient assessment, including life threats, medical history, vital signs, and targeted physical exam.

Once the patient assessment has been completed, periodic monitoring can help a rescuer track the improvement, stabilization, or decline in a patient's condition. Be conservative in your decision-making: It can be challenging to evacuate a patient from a remote location, so it is paramount to get moving toward help while the patient is still ambulatory.

ASSESSING PAIN

The OPQRST sequence of letters is a memory aid that can help to objectively record a patient's pain and similar complaint(s):

- **Onset** of the symptom, including the timing and activity of the onset
- **Provocation or palliation:** whether movement or pressure worsens or improves the symptom
- **Quality** of the symptom (e.g., sharp, dull, throbbing; intermittent or constant)
- **Radiating or referring pain**
- **Severity** on a scale of 1 to 10
- **Time** that the symptom began and how it has progressed

In this case, while the initial assessment did not reveal any definitive illness or evacuation urgency, the ranger monitored the patient as he descended toward base camp. As the inflammation of the appendix worsened and the patient's presentation exacerbated, the likely culprit and need for evacuation became more apparent. (*Source: Denali Mountaineering Rangers.*)

CARDIAC EMERGENCY: *A 57-year-old male was evacuated from 14,200-foot camp on May 16 after presenting at the medical tent with sudden-onset chest and left shoulder pain. He was treated for acute coronary symptom with oxygen, aspirin, and morphine and evacuated by helicopter, with an automated external defibrillator (AED) on board, later that afternoon.*

In such cases, the potential for further deterioration and myocardial infarction (heart attack) are too great to risk self-evacuation. If weather is not conducive to air rescue or helicopter transport is not available, care should be taken to minimize/eliminate exertion by the patient and evacuate by ground rescue. (Source: Denali Mountaineering Rangers.)

CREVASSE FALL AND 16-HOUR RESCUE | Climbing Unroped
Denali, West Buttress

At approximately 11:30 p.m. on June 4, an unroped climber fell into a crevasse just below the 7,800-foot camp on the West Buttress Route. The climber fell approximately 60 feet before coming to rest where the crevasse narrowed to about 12 inches in width. Numerous rangers, guides, and other climbers worked for roughly 15 hours to extricate the climber from the crevasse. He was severely hypothermic and sustained a brachial plexus nerve injury in one arm. He was flown by park helicopter directly to Fairbanks Memorial Hospital soon after extrication.

Looking down the narrow crevasse where an unroped climber spent 16 hours before he could be freed, severely hypothermic, by rangers using power tools. *Jake Beren*

This 38-year-old climber was on a private climbing expedition with six other teammates who flew onto the Kahiltna Glacier on May 21 and summited via the West Buttress Route on June 3. During their descent to base camp, the team divided into two groups, with five climbers on skis and two on snowshoes. Prior to his crevasse fall, the patient was traveling on snowshoes with one other teammate—the two were not roped together.

Shortly after passing through 7,800-foot camp, the two climbers encountered a four-foot-wide crevasse. As the first climber began to cross the snow bridge covering this crevasse, the bridge collapsed and caused the climber to fall roughly 60 feet, only stopping when he became wedged in the narrowing fissure. His partner could not see him and returned to the 7,800-foot camp to get help.

Multiple guides (Bill Allen, Kristie Kayl, Erin Laine, and Karl Welter) responded to the calls for help and notified mountaineering ranger Joe Reichert of the situation. The guides arrived on scene shortly after midnight and were able to communicate with the patient. These guides took turns descending into the crevasse multiple times to attempt extrication. The patient was wedged in such a way that simply hauling on his climbing harness would have resulted in further injury. The guides were able to clip into the patient's harness (in hopes of keeping him in place) and remove items from his backpack to allow additional room for him to breathe.

When the weather cleared at 3:55 a.m., the NPS helicopter was able to bring mountaineering rangers Dan Corn, Chris Erickson, Frank Preston, and two NPS volunteers to the accident scene to relieve the guides, who had been working continuously for almost four hours. The rescuers found the working conditions inside the crevasse to be extremely challenging. After lowering to the scene, each rescuer chipped away at the ice with an ice axe to create more room to extricate the patient. This process began about eight feet above the climber, where the crevasse

Mountaineering ranger Chris Erickson being lowered into the crevasse with a chainsaw to widen a constriction trapping the climber. *Jake Beren*

first narrowed to about a foot in width. At 4:45 a.m., Erickson was able to free the patient from his backpack and alleviate continued breathing issues.

More guides, mountaineering ranger Mik Shain, and NPS volunteers Jake Beren and Steve Gately arrived throughout the morning hours to assist in the rescue. A helicopter carrying rescuers from Talkeetna also brought tools requested from the Talkeetna Fire Department (chainsaw, pneumatic chisel, blowtorch) when it was realized that traditional mountaineering tools were not sufficient. The chainsaw was most useful at the crevasse lip, helping to open up the entry, and the pneumatic chisel was most effective at opening up the area above and surrounding the patient. The patient's snowshoes had become wedged and required the most effort to extract from the ice.

The patient was finally freed at 3:20 p.m. During the rescue, his mental status had steadily declined, to the point where he was responsive only to pain stimuli.

Once freed, the patient was raised from the crevasse with a mechanical advantage system and arrived on the glacier surface at 3:35 p.m., about 16 hours after he had fallen. The patient was transferred to a vacuum mattress for spinal-injury precautions and then flown in the NPS helicopter to Fairbanks Memorial Hospital. (The decision to fly north toward Fairbanks was dictated by inclement weather to the south of the mountain range.) The patient was treated in the ICU for several days, primarily for severe hypothermia, before being discharged to return home.

ANALYSIS

Traveling in glaciated terrain without a rope is never without risk. The snow bridges that cover crevasses degrade over time and can fail suddenly, as in this instance. Moreover, there is a heuristic trap that occurs when numerous people cross a bridge successfully, leading subsequent climbers to believe it is solid and safe. Being roped to teammates that can arrest an unexpected fall is the only way to prevent accidents like this from occurring. It's like a form of insurance where the cost is minimal and the benefits can be great.

The other factor highlighted by this accident was the wedging of the patient at the bottom of the crevasse as it narrowed. It is very unlikely that traditional companion-rescue techniques and tools would have extricated this climber before he succumbed to hypothermia. A similar incident occurred in the Alaska Range in the early 1980s, involving a climbing party of two, and the patient perished at the bottom of a crevasse when the partner was unable to free his partner. (*Source: Denali Mountaineering Rangers.*)

CREVASSE FALL AND SHOULDER DISLOCATION: *At approximately 5 a.m. on July 14, a guide called the NPS office in Talkeetna to report that a 33-year-old male climber had fallen eight to ten meters into a crevasse at 7,800 feet on the Kahiltna Glacier. The climber's rope team was able to arrest the fall, but he had dislocated his left shoulder. The patient was extricated to the surface after 20 to 30 minutes in the crevasse and flown to Talkeetna. (Source: Denali Mountaineering Rangers.)*

ALTITUDE ILLNESS (HAPE AND HACE)
Denali, West Buttress

On June 16, a 28-year-old male climber died from suspected high altitude pulmonary and cerebral edema (HAPE and HACE) at approximately 17,500 feet, while descending the West Buttress Route. Reports from his teammates revealed that he had struggled with altitude illness on previous high-altitude expeditions, including evacuations from both Aconcagua and Everest.

Despite the patient having a productive cough indicative of HAPE, the climber and his two partners departed for the summit on June 15, the ninth day of their expedition. The patient struggled to keep up and requested to remain at the Football Field, at approximately 19,500 feet, while his partners continued to the summit. His teammates reported that when they rejoined the patient, he was moving slowly and unsteadily. They began short-roping the climber below Denali Pass. The patient became non-ambulatory about 30 minutes above high camp, and his teammates secured him to an ice axe before descending to summon help. Another party on the route encountered this team and used a satellite device to initiate a rescue.

Mountaineering ranger Mark Westman, NPS volunteers, and five guides in the 17,200-foot camp responded. At the time of their callout, Westman reported, "the weather conditions were challenging, with extreme wind chill and near zero visibility." As NPS volunteers Pat Gault and Sam Luthy, the first rescuers on the scene, began constructing anchors for a lowering operation, the patient began removing his gloves and other attire, a behavior often characteristic of hypothermia, and his mental status deteriorated toward unresponsiveness.

The rescue team completed a 120-meter lower to get the patient to the flats near 17,200-foot camp. Then, while being carried toward camp, the patient deteriorated to both respiratory and cardiac arrest. The team attempted rescue breathing interventions, which were unsuccessful at reviving the patient. After a lack of respiration, pulse, and pupil response were confirmed, and with the continued extreme weather conditions, the decision was made to discontinue care.

ANALYSIS
Rarely does severe high-altitude illness present without warning signs. Based on the reports of teammates and nearby expeditions, this climber began exhibiting signs and symptoms of altitude illness as low as 11,200-foot camp. Continuing to ascend in spite of altitude illness almost guarantees continued or worsening illness. Mild altitude illness typically can be treated by remaining at the current elevation until it resolves, while patients with severe altitude illness (HAPE and HACE) should descend immediately. *(Source: Denali Mountaineering Rangers.)*

SNOW BLINDNESS

Denali, Cassin Ridge

On the evening of June 11, mountaineering rangers Melis Coady, Dave Weber, and Mark Westman responded to a 24-year-old male climber suffering from snow blindness at 14,200-foot camp. The climber had summited Denali via the Cassin Ridge one day earlier. The climb had been completed in poor weather with high winds. During their ascent, the team had lost multiple pieces of equipment, included the patient's goggles. This loss proved problematic on summit day when his glacier glasses didn't provide enough protection.

When continual treatment over a 24-hour period by NPS volunteer paramedics Jaime Anderson and Gabe Webster yielded no improvement, it was decided to evacuate this climber by helicopter. He was flown to Talkeetna on June 13, transferred to a local ambulance, and treated at Matsu Regional Hospital in Palmer.

ANALYSIS

Snow blindness can occur with surprisingly limited exposure to reflective glare at altitude. Some eye-specific ointments can help reduce the associated discomfort, but only time will heal this "sunburn" of the eye. The ailment requires rest with closed eyes in a shaded environment until healed. Unfortunately, prior to NPS involvement, a well-intentioned climber in camp treated this patient with a petro-

SNOW BLINDNESS – *Prevention and Treatment*

Snow blindness, or photokeratitis, is sunburn of the cornea and conjunctiva caused by ultraviolet (UV) light reflected by the snow surface.

PREVENTION

- Wear adequate eye protection even on cloudy days (glacier sunglasses, with side shields, or goggles with 100 percent UV protection). Carry backup protection.
- Minimize time without eye protection in glare-prone environments. Beware of removing icy or fogged-up sunglasses. Snow blindness can occur in as little as two hours of exposure.

SIGNS & SYMPTOMS

- Eye pain, eye redness, and tearing; vision difficulties; light sensitivity
- Signs and symptoms may be delayed up to 12 hours from exposure

TREATMENT PRINCIPLES

- Keep eyes closed and avoid bright light and further UV exposure (consider eye patches)
- Consider pain medications
- Symptoms typically resolve within one or two days with eye rest

leum-based ointment not intended for eye treatment and potentially increased the severity of this patient's issues. (*Source: Denali Mountaineering Rangers.*)

AVALANCHE AND KNEE INJURY
Denali, West Buttress, Rescue Gully

On the afternoon of June 16, a 28-year-old male triggered and was subsequently caught in an avalanche while skiing the Rescue Gully, below 17,200-foot camp on the West Buttress Route. During a tumbling fall of approximately 200 feet, the skier came to a rest atop the avalanche debris. However, he had lost his skis, various pieces of mountaineering equipment, and his prescription eyewear during the avalanche. The skier's team was able to evacuate him to 14,200-foot camp, where he was assessed and treated by NPS personnel. The skier was evacuated on June 17 in the NPS helicopter.

ANALYSIS
This zone is somewhat difficult to evaluate for avalanche hazard because skiers and climbers often will enter the gully from an adjacent ridge rather than climbing it from below. Moreover, the angle steepens and the couloir widens significantly once people exit the access chute and enter the main Rescue Gully. (*Source: Denali Mountaineering Rangers.*)

SHOULDER INJURY DURING SELF-ARREST
Denali, West Buttress

On June 21, a 58-year-old male climber injured his right shoulder during a self-arrest to stop a roped teammate's sliding fall on the ridge above 16,200 feet on the West Buttress Route. At 14,200-foot camp, the patient was examined and the shoulder determined to be unusable for a safe descent on foot. The patient was flown to Talkeetna to seek further treatment.

ANALYSIS
A sudden self-arrest creates violent twisting forces that can lead to injury. It's possible to minimize these impacts by staying mentally prepared for the possibility of self-arrest and by keeping minimal slack in the rope between teammates. (*Source: Denali Mountaineering Rangers.*)

THE MISLOW-SWANSON DENALI PRO AWARD: Given annually by the Talkeetna ranger staff, the Mislow-Swanson Denali Pro Award honors climbers demonstrating the highest standards of safety, self-sufficiency, Leave No Trace ethics, and assistance to fellow mountaineers. In 2017, the award went to five guides from the Alaska Mountaineering School: Wesley Bunch, Larry Holmgren, Lexie Hunsaker, Jake Kayes, and Chris Welch. These five were instrumental in the rescue attempt of a Nepalese climber who succumbed to altitude illness above the 17,200-foot high camp during the early morning hours of June 16. (See report on previous pages.) The guides assisted ranger Mark Westman's patrol for six hours in extremely adverse weather conditions, at altitude, and in a near zero-visibility whiteout.

CALIFORNIA

MT. SHASTA ANNUAL SUMMARY
Mt. Shasta and Castle Crags Wilderness

In 2017 there were four climbing-related incidents on Mt. Shasta. One accident was the result of rockfall, while the other three were primarily due to poor preparation for the terrain and environment.

Rescuers carry out a patient low on Shasta. *Nick Meyers*

On April 23, a party of three male climbers attempted to summit Shasta via the Avalanche Gulch route but turned back at the top of Red Banks. They descended to Horse Camp together, arriving safely in the afternoon. As they continued down toward Bunny Flat, one member (age 29) began to fall behind. The others told him to follow their tracks, but he ended up spending the night out with little gear (a very light pack, a lightweight puffy jacket, and snow pants). The climber was found on the morning of the 24th by another party and assisted down. He was uninjured.

This incident easily could have been avoided with proper preparation and better communication and teamwork; a map and compass and knowledge of how to use them would have gotten the lost climber to the trailhead. It is to be noted that the three climbers had just recently met on Facebook and were not regular climbing partners.

A 24-year old female climber sustained frostbite on May 14 during an attempt on the Avalanche Gulch route. The climber's boots had become wet during two days of snow camping and skills practice, and remained so during the summit attempt. After climbing for three hours in very cold temperatures (-10°F at 1 a.m.) and six or seven inches of fresh snow, the climber reported that she had no feeling in either of her feet. Realizing that she was at risk for cold injury, the party descended from 11,200 feet and sought medical care. She was diagnosed with mild frostbite to toes on both feet.

Prevention of frostbite injuries begins with dry and non-constrictive gear. Proper-fitting clothing that is layered will help to prevent overheating and sweating. Wet socks, gloves, and other clothing should be changed as soon as practical. Cold or numb extremities should be rewarmed through skin-to-skin contact. (Rewarming of frostbitten tissue in the field should only be done if there is no possibility of the injured site refreezing.)

On July 2, U.S. Forest Service climbing rangers, in conjunction with two local guides and a California Highway Patrol (CHP) helicopter, rescued an injured male climber in Avalanche Gulch below the Red Banks. The climber (male, mid-30s) was struck on the back of the head by rockfall that precipitated a 100-foot fall down the slope. He was found unconscious. The climber was stabilized and, after a hoist rescue, transported to Mercy Medical Center at Mt. Shasta.

On July 26, a 36-year-old female climber attempted to climb Shasta via the Clear Creek route. She and her partner got a late start and were inadequately prepared, both in knowledge and equipment, for a summit bid. After separating from her partner, who returned to their camp lower on the mountain, the climber continued to approximately 13,000 feet. At 10:39 p.m. she called 911 and requested assistance. As she was uninjured and rescuers would take a minimum of eight hours to reach her, she was instructed to find a safe location and to shelter in place until the morning.

The following day, Forest Service climbing rangers met the partner at the two women's campsite and pinged the missing climber's cell phone in an attempt to obtain her location. The climber's partner informed the rangers that the missing climber was dressed only in a neon green dress, light hiking boots, and a small pink windbreaker.

A full search and rescue operation was conducted throughout July 27 and 28 and included air assets from the National Guard and members of the Marin County, Contra Costa County, Josephine County, Jackson County, Bay Area Mountain Rescue, and Shasta County SAR teams. This search continued until the evening of July 28, when a 911 call was received from a different party who had found the missing climber. She was uninjured and escorted from the mountain.

Two incidents on Mt. Shasta in 2017 involved knee injuries to skiers, one of whom slid 100 to 200 feet after falling on icy, sun-cupped snow in Avalanche Gulch. (*Source: Mt. Shasta and Castle Crags Wilderness 2017 Climbing Ranger Report.*)

EDITOR'S NOTE: *There were nine searches and rescues of all types on Shasta (including self-rescues)—the fifth year in a row of relatively few incidents compared with the average of the previous 15 years. (A total of 6,817 summit passes were sold for Shasta in 2017, just above the 20-year average.) Nick Meyers, lead climbing ranger and director of the Mt. Shasta Avalanche Center, attributes this trend in part to good luck with climbing conditions and weather, but also to a sustained campaign of climber education, both on and off the mountain. Rangers offer clinics on climbing Shasta at California REI stores, and Meyers said far more climbers are checking recent conditions online (Shastaavalanche.org) before their attempts. During face-to-face contacts, the four climbing rangers "hammer the basics": 1) Ice axe use and quick and proper self-arrest, 2) Proper glissade technique, 3) Consequences of climbing into a whiteout, and 4) Dangers of party separation.*

Mt. Shasta rangers at the Helen Lake base camp.
Nick Meyers Collection

GROUND FALL | Protection Pulled Out
South Lake Tahoe, Lover's Leap

The Line (5.9), a popular traditional route, has been on my tick list for a couple of years. There's normally a conga line of climbers at the base, so my partner, Ben (30) and I (30) woke early on July 2 to make sure we were the first ones on the route. I had been climbing a lot, so I was confident that the route would be well within my abilities. I racked up quickly with only a brief check of the beta for which cams to bring. I didn't read the route description in detail, which said that the crux was 20 feet off the deck and difficult to protect.

The first 15 feet was very easy terrain (<5.6). I remember skipping a placement, thinking that it was too close to the ground and wouldn't do anything in a fall, and that there was no way I was going to fall. About 20 to 25 feet above the ground, the jugs disappeared, and I realized I was at the crux. I fiddled around, trying to get a piece into a small flared crack until I was satisfied with the placement of a 0.3/0.4 Black Diamond X4 Offset. The crux above the piece consisted of thin, slippery 5.9 face moves. I started getting nervous because I was expecting a crack crux—I was less confident in my face climbing than my crack climbing.

Because the cam was right at my feet and I thought it was a great placement, I decided to just go for it. As I began to make the move, my foot slipped. I started falling and watched as the cam popped out of the rock. I hit the ground (luckily missing some boulders) and presumably landed on my right side, with my right wrist absorbing most of the impact. I rolled several feet before stopping.

Luckily, there was a wilderness EMT waiting to get on the climb who assessed my injuries while another climber called 911. Due to the amount of pain in my wrist as well as some pain in my lower spine, I could not hike out. I ended up being airlifted to a nearby trauma center where I learned that I had not broken my back but had shattered my right wrist, broke my left thumb, and had a mild concussion.

ANALYSIS
There are a number of things I could have done differently, with the most important being that I should have done more research on the climb. If I had, I would have known that the crux was face climbing, not crack climbing, and that it had ground-fall potential, so I probably should not have skipped the lower placement. I did not extend my only piece with a quickdraw or sling, so it's possible that the cam got dislodged from its original placement. I also could have placed a backup piece in the crack. Finally, one should never just "go for it" in trad climbing—no piece is 100 percent bomber. (*Source: Jean C.*) *Editor's note: This particular route has seen a number of ground falls, including one earlier this year (2018), suggesting leaders who are near their limit should be taking additional care to protect the crux moves.*

LOWERING ERROR | Rope Too Short For Climb
South Lake Tahoe, Sugarloaf

On the afternoon of December 22, Nicholas C. (29) led Dominion, a 5.10a crack. After pulling the crux and moving through 30 feet of easy 5th-class terrain, Nicholas reached a set of bolted anchors and rigged to lower. He asked his belayer, Robert H.

ESSENTIALS

LOWER LEG INJURIES
ASSESSMENT AND TREATMENT

By R. Bryan Simon

Among the most common sites for traumatic climber injuries are the lower leg and ankle. These injuries are also likely to cause the need for evacuation and a visit to the hospital. Injuries to the lower leg range in severity from a sprained ankle to an open fracture. The following assessment and treatment techniques can be performed to assist an injured climber if a fall resulting in injury occurs.

ASSESSMENT

Always check for life-threatening injuries and address these first—think ABCs (airway, breathing, circulation) as well as head trauma and massive bleeding.

Common signs and symptoms of lower leg/ankle injury include pain, deformity, tenderness, crepitus (crackling or popping sound when touched or moved), rapid swelling or bruising, inability to bear weight on the injured leg, and loss of normal movement. Of these, the most common are pain, tenderness, and swelling. It is important to remember that not all serious injuries result in ankle deformity, including fractures of the talus (a spongy bone located directly below the tibia/fibula).

In order to assess the injury, remove climbing shoes, approach shoes, or mountaineering boots. (You may want to integrate approach shoes/boots into a splint later, but tight climbing shoes can cause further injury.) Once shoes and socks are removed, the most important items to check on any injured extremity are circulation, sensation, and movement (CSM).

Circulation. Finding a pulse in the feet is difficult. The dorsalis pedis artery is found on the top and outside of the prominent ridge of the foot while the posterior tibial artery is located behind the bone (medial malleolus) that sticks out on the inside of the ankle. If you are unable to find pulses at either site, try pinching the climber's toe. The nail bed will turn white, but a normal pink color will return within three seconds if there is normal blood flow.

Sensation. An injured extremity should be tested for both sharp and dull sensation. A pine needle works well for testing sharp sensation, while using the flat edge of your thumb is useful for the dull sensation. Try not to allow the climber to see which you are testing.

Movement. Ask the climber to wiggle the toes on the injured foot.

If the climber fails any of these tests, the injury is serious and immediate evacuation should occur. A loss of CSM could result in permanent injury.

Test whether the person can bear weight by having him or her try to take five steps. If they can, it is likely a sprain. If they cannot, it is indicative of a fracture. If your climbing partner cannot bear weight, it is better to be cautious and evacuate.

TREATMENT

If the injury is minor, the climber may only need to "RICE": **R**est, **I**ce, **C**ompression, and **E**levation. If you have ibuprofen, it can be helpful to reduce inflammation. If the climber cannot place body weight on the injured limb, there is deformity, or a lack of any component of CSM, the injury should be splinted and the climber evacuated.

A SAM splint—a foam-padded, malleable aluminum splint—is lightweight and highly effective, and some climbers carry one in their packs. If a SAM splint is unavailable, use whatever material is available. The tape splint and the U splint are easy to build (see below). Always check for CSM before and after placing a splint, and every 30 minutes thereafter. Get input from the injured climber regarding comfort and effectiveness of the splint.

The Tape Splint. An ACE bandage (found in many first-aid kits) is ideal, but if one is not available, two-inch climber's tape works well. It should be placed on the bare leg. Attempt to align the foot and leg in a 90° angle, but do NOT do so if this causes an increase in pain. Begin taping on top of the foot, just above the big toe, and wrap to the inside and under the ball of the foot and then around and above the foot to

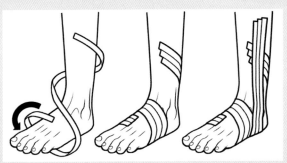

When placing any type of splint, be sure to check for comfort and support of the injury. Replacing the boot or shoe after completing the splint, if possible, adds protection and stability. Quiregraphics.com

the inside of ankle, anchoring the tape strip below the calf. Repeat three times with strips of tape side by side. Next, using additional tape, attach one end to the interior of the mid-calf and run directly under the heel and anchor tape to exterior of the leg at mid-calf. Repeat three times. This splint limits the movement of the ankle in all directions.

Improvised U-Splint. Using whatever clothing is available, roll it tightly into a tube. If using a shirt, roll from neck to the bottom of the shirt. Position the foot to as near as 90° as possible (without increasing pain) and position the roll at the center of the sole of the foot. Take the two ends and use tape to secure them just above the ankle and on the lower leg.

EVACUATION

If you suspect a fracture, get your partner to the nearest medical center. If there is loss of any component of CSM, evacuation should be hastened, as permanent damage may occur.

REFERENCE

Vertical Aid: Essential Wilderness Medicine for Climbers, Trekkers, and Mountaineers, by Seth Hawkins, R. Bryan Simon, Pearce Beissinger, and Deb Simon (2017).

R. Bryan Simon, R.N., is senior editor of this publication.

(52), for tension and began to descend. At approximately 40 feet above the ground, the tail of the rope passed through the belayer's device and the climber fell to the ground, sustaining a number of injuries, including compound pilon fractures of both ankles, a fractured coccyx, a compression fracture of the T12 vertebrae, and a laceration of the chin. A helicopter rescue was not possible because of darkness, so Nicholas was carried out in an evacuation that lasted 3.5 hours and required the cutting of a new trail to accommodate the litter.

ANALYSIS

Nicholas C. writes: "The past two times we had climbed this route, most recently about four years earlier, we had used a 70-meter rope, and I was able to lower directly below the route and make it to a point where I could downclimb. This route can be climbed with a 60m rope, but you need to swing to climber's right when lowering to make it to an easy downclimb. I should have read the beta on the descent prior to climbing to refresh my memory, rather than being complacent in the fact that I had done the route before.

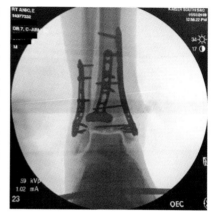

Repairs after the Sugarloaf accident.

Obviously, a stopper knot would have prevented this, and if the belayer kept an eye on the halfway point we would have had a greater awareness of the rope remaining." (*Source: Nicholas C.*)

STRANDED | Failure to Rappel, Inexperience
Yosemite Valley, Royal Arches

On March 3, at 8:24 p.m., two male climbers (both in their early 20s) reported they were stranded partway up the Royal Arches route (approximately 15 pitches, 5.7 C0). The climbers had moved slower than expected, and, with a storm approaching, they decided to rappel the route with a single rope after the pendulum traverse on pitch 10. After two rappels, the climbers found themselves without fixed rappel anchors and were unable to continue.

Cold and tired, and with bad weather moving in fast, they decided to call YOSAR. They were instructed to stay put and continually exercise to stay warm. (The climbers had food, water, and jackets.) By the time the SAR team had mobilized, rain had begun falling in earnest and it became unsafe for them to conduct a rescue that night. Once the storm cleared, two SAR team members climbed to the stranded climbers, reaching them at 11 a.m., and rappelled with them to the ground.

ANALYSIS

There are abundant opportunities for building gear rappel anchors on and around the Royal Arches route. Be willing to leave equipment for anchors when making un-

Approximate line of the Royal Arches Route, showing (1) the start of the standard rappel route and (2) the rappel route attempted by the stranded climbers. *Mark Roth*

planned rappels. Bringing two ropes on a long climb will decrease the number of rappels necessary in a retreat and increases your chances of finding fixed anchors or anchor-building opportunities. It's also important to have the equipment and knowledge to reascend rappel ropes and choose an alternate rappel route if the first one leads to a dead-end.

These climbers headed up a long route with a storm in the forecast. They were lucky the storm wasn't colder or more prolonged, as a Sierra storm in March can quickly cause hypothermia. (*Source: Yosemite National Park Climbing Rangers.*)

OFF-ROUTE RAPPEL ON THE NOSE: *On the night of May 15, around midnight, two climbers (male and female, both in their 30s) reported they were stranded on a ledge below Dolt Tower on El Capitan. The climbers had attempted an alpine-style ascent of the Nose, bivying once at El Cap Tower. Moving more slowly than expected, and with a storm forecasted, they decided to retreat just short of the Great Roof at 5:30 p.m. on their second day of climbing.*

After a number of successful rappels, the team had rappelled from El Cap Tower and arrived at an anchor 50 feet right of Dolt Tower. From here, they rappelled to the next visible anchor, the top of pitch seven of the Central Scrutinizer, a hard aid climb adjacent to the Nose. Their last rappel of the day took them to a large ledge system, where they built a gear anchor and pulled their ropes with the hope that they would find rappel stations below. However, they were not successful, nor could they climb back up the line they had rappelled. Luckily, they were well prepared for an emergency bivy, with food, jackets, and water.

Next morning, using a spotting scope in El Cap Meadow, YOSAR determined the climbers would be able to reach a large corner system midway up pitch five on the Real Nose route, and from there a rappel route existed to the ground. By cell phone, they advised the team to rappel to this corner, build another gear anchor, and continue their descent from there.

There is a tremendous amount of information available for the Nose climb and a well-established rappel line. Haste may have contributed to the climbers' decision to commit to their gear anchor on what should have been a bolted rappel route. (Source: Yosemite National Park Climbing Rangers.)

FALL ON ROCK | Inadequate Protection, Fatigue
Yosemite Valley, El Capitan, Salathé Wall

The period from May 11–19 delivered a mix of spring weather to Yosemite. Cameron Brown (age 41) and I (Stephen Shostek, age 59) experienced sun, rain, snow, and cold weather during our Salathé Wall climb. We sheltered for two days in the Alcove (pitch 20) during a storm. Our climb was slower and longer than we expected due to the storm and wet conditions, so we were stretching our food supply.

We spent our final night on Long Ledge after a long day—I finished cleaning the Headwall at 2:30 a.m. Next morning I started aiding the pitch above Long Ledge, mostly on small cams and offset cams, up to the flaring scar where a fixed pin shown on the topo formerly had resided. I pounded a cam hook into the flaring pin scar with the heel of my hand. As I weighted the cam hook, a few grains of granite fell from the crack, so I figured the hook wouldn't hold for long in the flare. As I assessed the 5.10 free moves required to move leftward to easier ground, the cam hook pulled, the Metolius offset placed in the flaring crack below pulled, and my fall was arrested by a Metolius 00 Master Cam in a parallel section of the thin crack. My 25-foot fall was clean and caused no problems.

I aided back up to the Metolius 00, seated it deeper into the crack, replaced the offset cam that had pulled from the flare and aided up on it, and again pounded in the cam hook with the heel of my hand. I saw another, smaller pin scar in the seam two feet higher and placed another cam hook in this flaring scar, hoping it might hold my weight more securely. However, the higher cam hook failed while I was testing it, as did the lower cam hook and the offset cam, and this time the 00 Master Cam also pulled out of the crack. I had back-cleaned some offset cams in the flaring crack above a 0.3 Camalot much farther down the crack, since they appeared to be useless to arrest a fall. My fall was finally stopped by the 0.3 Camalot.

I fell about 50 feet, and near the bottom my left foot snagged on a protruding fin of granite. I suffered an avulsion fracture of my left fibula at the talofibular ligament attachment, soft-tissue damage to my left ankle and foot, and an avulsion of the distal attachment of the extensor tendon on my left pinkie finger.

Cameron lowered me back to Long Ledge, and we assessed our options. I was unable to reclimb the pitch with my injured left ankle, but reasoned that I was able to jug a rope with one good foot. Luckily, Alex Honnold and James Lucas were passing above us on Freerider, and they offered to fix our rope and help us haul our gear up the final two pitches. I jugged to the top and assessed that my injured ankle was able to bear some weight tolerably if I carefully weighted only the heel area, so I resolved to get down the East Ledges descent without calling for rescue assistance. I limped, crab crawled, and butt slid down to the rappels and out the trail to the road.

ANALYSIS

There are a few things I could have done differently to prevent my accident and injury. The thin crack where I placed the Metolius 00 is parallel sided, unlike the flaring crack below. I should have added another cam and equalized them in the relatively secure parallel portion of the crack. Likewise, the flaring placement for the offset cam might have been able to hold a fall if I'd equalized additional cams.

Climber QX Cheang (unrelated to this incident) starting up the tricky pitch off Long Ledge on the Salathé Wall. *Kelly Khiew*

I also might have tried placing offset nuts in the flaring crack below the Metolius 00.

Fatigue played a role in my accident. I was aware of feeling dull-minded when I started the pitch due to inadequate sleep, reduced food rations, and burning additional calories in the cold weather. With sharper cognition, it's likely that I would have backed up the micro-cam. It's also possible that I would have launched more quickly into the 5.10 free climbing above the missing fixed pin and thus avoided the fall. [*Editor's note: This pitch is rated 5.8 C1+ in some guidebooks, but is generally considered to be significantly harder—many say it is the crux of the Salathé when done as an aid climb.*] Additionally, I had climbed this pitch once before, in 2000, and in retrospect I can see that I was overconfident about climbing it this time.

Months after the accident, I was back to climbing, although with some pain and reduced flexibility in my left ankle. My left pinkie is useful again but won't regain its full range of motion. I'm climbing with a more informed and careful approach. (*Source: Stephen Shostek.*)

RAPPEL ERROR | No Backups, No Helmet
Yosemite Valley, Glacier Point Apron, Monday Morning Slab

At 6:59 p.m. on June 10, Yosemite dispatch received a report that a climber had rappelled off the end of her rope while descending Harry Daley (2 pitches, 5.8). Barbara (mid-30s, not her real name) was now on top of the fourth-class pinnacle that marks the start of the climb. By the time YOSAR arrived on scene, Barbara's boyfriend (early 30s) had rappelled down to join Barbara on top of the pinnacle. Barbara was not wearing a helmet and had suffered major head trauma, but was alive and able to communicate with SAR personnel. The boyfriend told responders that she had lost consciousness for several minutes after the fall.

Once the SAR team stabilized and packaged Barbara in a litter, they lowered her from the pinnacle and carried her out to an ambulance at the parking area. She had multiple spinal and skull fractures, a broken nose, simple pneumothorax, a broken rib, and a number of more superficial injuries, but she lived.

ANALYSIS

To the best of her recollection, Barbara had been rappelling the second pitch of Harry Daley. She had descended about 10 to 15 feet past the usual belay stance atop the first pitch and swung left to pick up some equipment they had dropped while climbing. She retrieved both pieces, clipped them to her harness, and moved back right. After this, she stated, the last thing she remembers was noticing that there was not very much rope left below her tube-style rappel device.

The rappels from this two-pitch route can be done with two 60-meter ropes or a single 70-meter, but the first rappel is a stretcher with a 70. (It is believed the climbers were using a 70-meter rope.) Barbara did not have any knots tied in the ends of her rope, and did not have a hands-free backup. Barbara, who had six or seven years of climbing experience, five of which involved outdoor lead climbing, stated in a follow-up interview that she used to always tie knots in the ends of her rope while rappelling but stopped due to friends making fun of her.

A hands-free backup (such as an autoblock) might not have prevented this accident, but it would have given Barbara more control during this rappel. Because she has no memory of her fall. we don't know whether she simply rappelled off the end or lost control of the rope.

Finally, Barbara's head injuries may have been less severe had she been wearing a helmet. (*Source: Yosemite National Park Climbing Rangers.*)

LOWERING ERRORS | Ropes Too Short, Helmet/No Helmet
Yosemite Valley, Swan Slab and Church Bowl

On July 3 there were two climbing accidents almost identical in nature in the Valley. Both were ground falls, and both resulted from a belayer lowering the climber with a rope that was too short for the pitch.

At approximately 7 p.m., Yosemite dispatch received a report that a climber had fallen from the Swan Slab Gully (5.6). YOSAR and the Valley ambulance quickly arrived on scene. The first responders found a mid-20s male lying on the ground face up, being held by his climbing partner. While the climber was conscious, he was disoriented and struggling to stay awake. Furthermore, he was complaining of back and hip pain, and witnesses stated he may have hit his head. He did not have on a helmet. After the climber was assessed and packaged for transport, the rescue team carried him the short distance to the road, and he was evacuated from the Ahwahnee meadow by medical helicopter at approximately 8:10 p.m.

Other climbers in the area stated the climber, a beginner, was being lowered on top-rope when the end of the rope slipped through the belayer's device. It was determined in these interviews that the fall was around 25 feet. The climber's rope, measured by NPS employees, was only about 98 feet long. The route is about 60 feet high and would require at least 120 feet of rope to lower a climber from the bottom.

Immediately following the Swan Slab accident, Yosemite dispatch received a report of a ground fall at Church Bowl. The reporting party stated that the climber was on Black is Brown (5.9) and had fallen about 20 feet. YOSAR found a male climber in his mid-20s at the base of the climb. He complained of hip and back pain, but had suffered no loss of consciousness. The patient had a helmet, which had impacted the rock and cracked during the fall. The climber was assessed in the hospital and released that evening with no major injuries.

In interviews after the accident, it was determined that the climber was being lowered from a tree anchor after leading the climb. At approximately 20 feet off the ground, the end of the climber's rope passed through his partner's belay device. While one guidebook states that the climb is 80 feet tall, the anchor that the climber used was over 100 feet off the ground, requiring a 70-meter rope to lower or rappel all the way to the ground. The patient believed his rope to be 70 meters, but the SAR noted that the rope was visibly cut at both ends, and upon measuring they determined the rope to be about 62 meters. This was the first time the two climbers had met and was the patient's first climb in Yosemite.

ANALYSIS

Both of these accidents could have been avoided with some basic safety measures.

Close the belay system. A stopper knot at the belayer's end of the rope or tying the belayer into his or her end would have prevented both of these ground falls.

Know your rope, know your route. Both parties were climbing on ropes that had been intentionally cut to a shorter length. If you choose to modify your rope, know exactly how long it is and tell your climbing partners. And never blindly trust guidebooks. In the Church Bowl accident, the climber used an anchor that was roughly 30 feet higher than the guidebook's listed distance.

Both climbers impacted their heads during their falls. At Church Bowl, the climber's helmet was heavily damaged by the fall but he escaped serious injury. Without the helmet, the outcome could have been tragic. (*Source: Yosemite National Park Climbing Rangers.*)

DEADLY ROCKFALL
Yosemite Valley, El Capitan

On the afternoons of September 27 and 28, a series of rockfalls occurred on the far right side of El Capitan, near the line of Horsetail Fall. The initial rockfall on September 27 struck two climbers who were walking along the base of the cliff after retreating from the East Buttress route. One of the climbers, Andrew Foster, 32, from Wales, was killed by the rockfall. Witnesses reported that he had rushed to shield his wife from the debris when he was hit. She was seriously injured and was transported by short-haul helicopter rescue to El Cap Meadow and then to an area hospital for treatment.

Over four hours, six more rockfalls occurred, for a total volume of about 450 cubic meters (a cubic meter is about the size of a washing machine) or about 1,340 tons.

A much larger rockfall occurred in the same general area on September 28. This one measured 10,250 cubic meters in volume, or about 30,500 tons. The rockfall generally propagated upward and outward from the origin of the September 27 rockfall, greatly expanding the overall source area. Boulders reached the Valley floor, and smaller fragments traveled to Northside Drive. One piece struck a vehicle, hitting the driver and causing a head injury.

The September 28 rockfall ranks as the 29th largest on record in Yosemite. It had been 18 years since the last rockfall-related fatality in the park, when climber Peter Terbush was killed by a rockfall from Glacier Point on June 13, 1999.

Most rockfalls in Yosemite occur in the winter and early spring, during periods of intense rainfall, snowmelt, and/or subfreezing temperatures, but large rockfalls—like these ones from El Capitan—have occurred during periods of warm, stable weather.

How can climbers address rockfall risk? Unfortunately there are no hard or fast rules, but rockfall areas are often active for many hours, days, or even months, so avoid climbing in recent rockfall zones. The "progressive" nature of the El Cap rockfalls, with several events from the same location, has also been seen at other locations in Yosemite, including Middle Brother and the Rhombus Wall. Fresh talus and/or damaged vegetation at the base of your intended climb are good indicators of recent activity. Be especially aware of cracking or popping sounds emanating from the cliffs, as these sounds have preceded many rockfalls.

Rockfall on the right side of El Capitan in September 2017. The Waterfall Route, located in this area, has continued to shed rock in 2018. *NPS Photo*

A helmet may not save you from a large rockfall, but it could offer protection from "flyrock" that accompanies most rockfalls. Minimize your time approaching or bivying at the bases of cliffs, particularly those in known rockfall zones. (*Source: ClimbingYosemite.com/Yosemite National Park Climbing Rangers.*)

FALL ON ROCK | Speed Climbing, Inadequate Protection
Yosemite Valley, El Capitan, The Nose

On October 11, Quinn Brett (female, 30s) was attempting a Nose in a Day ascent with Josie McKee when she took a very long fall while leading the right side of the Boot Flake. The two women were using speed-climbing tactics: Brett was effectively roped soloing while McKee ascended a portion of their rope that had been fixed to the previous anchor, at the top of Texas Flake. Brett had back-cleaned several aid pieces between the top of the bolt ladder off Texas Flake and the bottom of Boot Flake, and she did not leave any protection in Boot Flake, a hand crack rated 5.10c. Consequently, when she fell, the fall distance was greater than 100 feet. She impacted the sloping left side of Texas Flake (her right scapula took the brunt of the fall) and came to a stop among some boulders lower down without the rope coming tight. She was wearing a helmet, but it came off during the fall or impact.

McKee, a veteran of YOSAR, rappelled to Brett, telephoned for help, and prepared the scene for a rescue. Rangers were heli-slung to the top of El Cap Tower, just below Texas Flake. They placed Brett in a litter, and she and a ranger were flown off the wall to El Cap Meadow. McKee and another ranger then rappelled to the ground.

ANALYSIS

Both Brett and McKee were expert climbers with numerous speed ascents (including speed records) on El Capitan and other walls. Brett does not remember exactly what caused her fall. She explained that when climbing Boot Flake during a speed ascent she normally would clip cams to semi-dynamic tethers attached to her harness, and she would back herself up with one or both cams as she climbed the hand crack. Just before the fall, she remembers removing a red (number 1) Camalot from the crack and watching it and the tether drop between her legs, but she isn't certain if she prepared or placed a larger cam on the other tether before falling—that is, whether a cam pulled out of the crack or if she was completely unprotected when she fell.

Speed climbing of big-wall routes often involves long runouts and tactics that shave safety margins razor-thin. Brett had climbed the Nose eight times before and had never fallen on Boot Flake. She survived a seemingly unsurvivable fall but suffered numerous injuries, the most serious of which was a burst fracture of the

Rescue helicopter prepares to fly Quinn Brett and a Yosemite ranger from Texas Flake on the Nose. Brett fell from the right side of Boot Flake, partially hidden behind the helicopter. *Tom Evans | El Cap Report*

12th thoracic vertebra, leading to paralysis from approximately the waist down. (*Source: The Editors.*)

Editor's note: An interview with Quinn Brett about this incident is featured in Episode 26 of the Sharp End Podcast.

BROKEN BACK ON HALF DOME: *In October, Alex Doria was injured in a long fall on the third pitch of the Regular Northwest Face on Half Dome. Doria had made a substantial runout to a stance near the end of the 5.8 pitch and was preparing to place a piece when he lost his balance and fell. He broke his L1 vertebra and bones in his foot and wrist. His climbing partner, Jonathan Wachtel, was able to get him to the base of the wall, from which he was evacuated by helicopter. Doria and Wachtel describe this incident in detail in Episode 29 of the Sharp End Podcast.*

FATAL FALL | Possible Rappel Error
Yosemite Valley, Fifi Buttress

On November 17 two friends of Niels Tietze hiked to the base of Fifi Buttress to look for their overdue friend. The two knew that Tietze had been up on the formation, working to establish a new route, and had been doing so alone, using fixed lines and self-belay techniques. It was late in the season and he was most likely removing his ropes and gear from the wall. Nobody had seen Tietze since earlier in the week, and he had missed climbing plans with friends the day before.

When the two arrived at the base of the cliff they discovered Tietze's body and immediately recognized that he had taken an unsurvivable climbing fall. At approximately 2 p.m. they notified SAR by cell phone.

At the scene, park rangers found Tietze wearing a climbing harness. His shoes were off, but there were two climbing shoes found nearby. He had climbing gear clipped to his harness, including cams, carabiners, and slings. There was also an adjustable wrench and round wire brush. A low-stretch, 254-foot rope was found strewn about the scene. The rope was not connected to the harness. There were no knots in the rope. The midway point was looped into one slot of a rappel device as if for a single-rope rappel. The retention cable of the friction device was broken. The rappel device was not attached to the locking carabiner found on the harness.

The carabiner attached to the harness belay loop had a screw lock with the screw in the locked position; however, the gate was effectively locked open because the nose of the carabiner was not captured by the screw lock.

Since Tietze was by himself at the time, no one can know for sure what happened. The findings at the scene suggest he might have accidentally weighted a rope set for a doubled-over rappel with only one strand of rope in the device and carabiner. However, the fact that the ATC and rope were not connected to his harness when he was found detract from this theory and could be explained only if they had managed to come out of the "locked open" carabiner during the fall.

A second option would be that an unknown event interrupted Tietze as he was rigging for rappel—after he passed the rope through the ATC but before the ATC was clipped to the carabiner in his belay loop. An attempt to grab the rope could explain how it made it to the ground. There is simply no way to know if this was the case.

The broken retention cable on his rappel device is unusual, but in and of itself would not have caused an accident to occur, as the retention cable does not assist in the operation of a plaquette device. The "locked open" carabiner certainly could have played a part in the accident. However, the fact that the middle mark of the rope was through his rappel device strongly suggests a rappel rigging error.

ANALYSIS

The following lessons are among those that can be drawn from this tragic incident:

- Always clip in directly to each anchor while preparing to rappel. Whether using a manufactured or home-rigged PAS (personal anchor system), a Purcell prusik, or the slings on hand, it is extremely important to attach yourself to the anchor while rigging for rappel.
- Test your system. After going in direct and rigging for rappel, weight and test your system before unclipping from the anchor. Verify that you have done everything correctly before trusting your life to a rappel.
- Always use a "third hand" backup. When you attach a third-hand backup such as a kleimheist or autoblock prior to loading your rappel device, you have a preliminary point of attachment to the rope. If all else fails, it could save your life.

- Be extra cautious when alone. No one else is there to check your systems, and no one is there in case of an accident.
- Beware complacency. Niels Tietze was a climber of the absolute highest caliber. He had spent years of his life rescuing people off the walls of Yosemite. It only takes one bad rappel after thousands of well-executed ones for something like this to happen. Stay sharp. (*Source: Yosemite National Park Climbing Rangers.*)

ROPED-SOLOING FALL | Protection Pulled out
Yosemite Valley, El Capitan, Zodiac

On the morning of December 2, I started up the first pitch of Zodiac (5.9 A3) on El Capitan. I was roped soloing and planning for three or four days on the wall. I had led this first pitch two other times.

I climbed the pitch clean (no pitons, C3+) and was about 10 feet from the anchor, underneath a small roof, when the small offset nut I was weighting blew out. As I fell, two marginal placements beneath me also pulled out. The next piece was a well-placed 0.75-sized cam. Surprisingly, this piece sheared out of the parallel, non-flaring granite crack. Below this was a well-placed nut, which somehow came unclipped from the rope. And below this was another 0.75-size cam—the carabiner clipped to this cam broke, presumably due to a "nose hook."

In all, six placements pulled out or otherwise failed, and I fell approximately

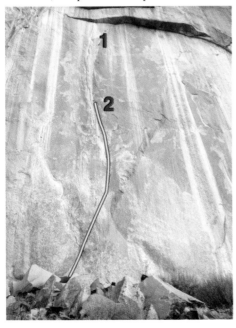

The first pitch of Zodiac, showing (1) climber's high point near the top belay anchor and (2) the highest piece of protection that held. The climber estimated he fell 110 feet. *Parker Kempf*

110 feet, stopping at eye level with the first bolt on the route. The aiders clipped to the ends of my daisies were touching the ground.

Remarkably, I sustained only a small scratch on one ankle and was otherwise uninjured. The Silent Partner I was using as a self-belay device had broken in the locked position and was no longer functional. Returning later with a friend to clean the rest of my gear from the route, we discovered the piece that caught my fall was a medium-size DMM offset stopper, which had half of its cable blown through. Had this piece failed, the fall surely would have been fatal.

ANALYSIS

I've done over 15 big-wall solos, including two roped solos of El Capitan. I bounce-test all my aid placements, even C1 placements in splitter cracks, just to be sure the piece does not shift out of its optimal placement. The first pitch of Zodiac gets very high traffic, which has led to an infamous amount of "polishing" in the crack. I certainly was not expecting a well-placed 0.75 to shear out of solid rock, but maybe the polish has reduced the rock friction so that a nut would have been more appropriate here.

It had not rained at all recently, but it was early morning in winter. Although I did not notice the rock was wet, it's possible there was dew or other moisture in the crack, exacerbating the polished rock issue. Again, passive protection would have probably held better at this placement. Perhaps it also would have helped to wait a little before starting and let any morning dew evaporate.

Because I was roped soloing, I was not using quickdraws or extending placements; my rope was fixed to a ground anchor, and I fed slack through the "brake side" of my solo belay device. (There is no rope being pulled through protection in a lead roped-solo scenario.) It's possible, though far from certain, that extending the "failed" pieces with quickdraws might have made the cam less likely to pull out, the nut less likely to come unclipped, and/or the carabiner less likely to break.

The broken carabiner, an old-style Camp Photon, had a distinct notch between end of the nose of the carabiner and the "basket." This notch was prone to snagging slings and other gear, and "nose hooking" significantly weakens a carabiner. Using a key-lock carabiner with a narrower angle to its basket would have helped keep the force of the fall along the spine of the carabiner. (*Source: Parker Kempf.*)

FATAL GROUND FALL | Rope Likely Cut Over Edge
Yosemite National Park, Matthes Crest

On July 30, at 1:59 p.m., Yosemite dispatch was notified via a 911 call that a climber (Matt Price, male, 20s) had fallen near the start of the classic south ridge of Matthes Crest. The reporting party (Jeff, also in his 20s) said he was Matt's climbing partner and had witnessed the fall, and that Matt had died.

Matt and Jeff had met in person only a few days prior to their climb, after striking up a friendship on an online climbers' forum. They had decided to meet for a climbing trip to Yosemite, and on Saturday, July 29, the two climbed Tenaya Peak. Jeff stated that they felt comfortable and seemed to be "really in sync."

On Sunday the 30th the two hiked to Matthes Crest from the Cathedral Lakes trailhead. They arrived at the base sometime before noon and prepared for the climb. They had brought two 60-meter, 8.5mm half ropes and discussed the pros and cons of using both simultaneously (as per design) or using just one to simplify rope management. They were both under the impression that a single-strand 8.5mm half rope could hold a leader fall safely, so they agreed to keep one rope in Matt's backpack and bring it out once they reached the rappels at the summit of the North Tower.

The team agreed to swing leads, with Jeff leading the first pitch. At the first belay stance, they prepared to swap leads and discussed strategy for the next pitch. The most frequently traveled route would have led slightly climber's left of the belay station but involved a spooky step-across move that made Matt uncomfortable. Another option to climber's right of the belay station appeared to consist of easy face climbing but with few protection options. Jeff later said that Matt

Area above the first belay on Matthes Crest. (1) Belay stance. (2) Leader's only protection (a slung horn). (3) Leader's approximate high point on the right side of a shallow arête, five to ten feet beyond the slung horn. The normal route moves left and up from the belay. *NPS Photo*

became increasingly nervous as they discussed the options; he offered to lower Matt to find a better route or even call off the climb. Matt decided he would take the climber's right option. Somewhere between noon and 1 p.m., he started climbing.

After several moves, Matt was able to sling a horn with a runner. He continued to climb up and right on the face. Jeff reported that his last words to Matt were, "Don't climb up anything you can't climb back down."

Matt reached a point about five to ten feet past his protection and out of Jeff's line of sight. Jeff heard him yell an expletive and could tell that he was falling. He felt a tug on his belay device and believed that he had successfully caught the fall. Within what he described as a second, he felt the tension on the rope release and saw Matt falling to the base of the route. Jeff yelled down several times without any response.

After several moments he pulled the rope back and saw that it had been broken or been cut. Jeff took several moments to establish a rappel anchor and then rappelled on the remaining rope to the base of the climb, where he found that Matt had died from his injuries.

Jeff attempted to call 911 numerous times but was unable to get a call through. He decided to hike to the north end of Matthes, about 1.5 miles away, where he eventually was successful in making a 911 call. He was instructed to return to the accident site and wait for rescue personnel. At approximately 5 p.m., SAR team members had arrived on scene at the base of Matthes Crest and confirmed that Matt had been killed in the fall. (*Source: Yosemite National Park Climbing Rangers.*)

ANALYSIS

Based on an examination of the rope and the site of the fall, it is likely the rope cut as it slid along one or more of the sharp flakes or crystals in the area. The victim was climbing an arête to the right of his only protection on the pitch, and the rope would have dragged along the face under tension as he fell. After the fall, about 20 feet of rope remained attached to the victim, plus about three feet of exposed core.

It's impossible to know if this accident would have occurred had the party been using both of the half ropes, or if they had been using a single-rated rope. Technical investigators who surveyed the scene stated that a larger rope might also have been cut in the same situation. Nonetheless, a climb such as this, especially early in one's climbing career, is no place to test the boundaries of one's equipment. When a rope system is tested and rated to be used a certain way, that is how it should be used.

The evidence suggests a rope cutting over an edge led to this fatality, but the climber's fall is what caused the rope to cut. While the two climbers seemed to be within their physical capabilities, a route like Matthes Crest may have been inappropriate for the team, based on their alpine experience. Finding the best line on this climb (as with many High Sierra climbs) requires route-finding skill; it's also important to have the ability to downclimb or traverse out of unexpected difficulties. Pushing your personal comfort zone is best done in less committing environments. (*Sources: Yosemite National Park Climbing Rangers and the Editors.*)

RAPPEL ERROR | Rappelled Off End of Rope in Storm
Yosemite National Park, Matthes Crest

My climbing partner and I were attempting to climb Tenaya Peak, Matthes Crest, and Cathedral Peak—three long but moderate routes in the Tuolumne Meadows area—in a day. Because of the sheer amount of climbing and distance we would need to travel, we packed light, opting not to carry any warm or waterproof layers.

We left our car at 6 a.m. and summited Tenaya at roughly 9:30 a.m., then hiked 3.5 miles over to Matthes Crest and began climbing around noon. About 2 p.m. we noticed what looked like thunderstorms far in the distance, but the clouds seemed to be moving away from us, so we continued. At 3 p.m., as we were nearing the south summit, we noticed clouds forming directly above us, so decided to bail and began searching for a descent. We found a gully on the west side, just before the south summit, that had slings around various trees in it. We scrambled down around 30 feet to the first tree anchor and began flaking our 60-meter rope.

Almost immediately, it began hailing and a lighting storm started directly on top of us. In such an exposed position, we were shaken and began rushing. Rather than properly flaking the rope out and finding the midpoint (our rope did not have a middle marker), I tied knots in both ends and sent my partner down the rappel immediately, figuring we needed to get below the top. Before reaching the next rappel tree (only about 40 feet below), he had to stop and untangle the rope and reposition the rope ends, which took some time.

Eventually, he made it to the next tree anchor and I quickly descended to join him. Dime-size hail was falling, and lightning was all around us. In my haste, I didn't move the rappel lines out of the constricted gully we were rappelling and onto the face. When we went to pull the rope, it became stuck. Luckily, I also had brought a 65-meter static tag line. So, while my partner continued to try to free the stuck rope, I began uncoiling the thin tag line. It almost immediately tangled. Again, opting for speed over thoroughness, I eyeballed what I thought was the midpoint and tossed the ends down. In my haste, I only tied a stopper knot in one end.

As I began to rappel, I had to stop multiple times to pull the loose ends of the rope out of the waterfall-filled gully. After about 25 meters, I reached the base of the vertical wall and was standing on a 45-degree slab. Feeling confident that I had made it down to scrambling terrain, I began scouting for a good stance to go off rappel. As I descended a few more feet, the unknotted end of the rope slipped through my ATC and my autoblock and I began tumbling. I rolled 50 feet down a tiered rock slab before finally coming to a stop.

Miraculously, I survived relatively unscathed. My helmet was dented, and I had large gashes in my left knee and right arm, but no concussion, broken bones, or other serious injuries. Also, I had not pulled the tag line down with me when I fell, so my partner was able to reset the rappel (properly this time) and rappel down to me.

We had no cell phone service, no warm or dry gear, and were about six miles from the closest trailhead. We had a bivy sack with us, but decided it would be better to keep moving rather than wait out the storm. Leaving the ropes behind, we started hiking. Six hours later, at 9:30 p.m., we reached the trailhead and someone offered us a ride back to our car at Tenaya Lake, from which we drove to the closest ER.

Looking northward along Matthes Crest. The climbers in this incident descended to the left (west) before reaching the first summit. *Roman Smart*

ANALYSIS

I am acutely aware that rappelling accidents typically don't end this well. One conclusion you might take away from this account is that people should recommit to perfect rappelling practices: Always tie stopper knots, always make sure the midpoint of the rope is at the anchor, always use a backup, etc. I agree wholehearted with these practices, but in a crisis even well-trained people are prone to making mistakes. The real lessons for me are how to avoid a crisis situation in the first place.

To that end, I think there are several takeaways. First, we were in the high-country, far from any road, and it was utterly irresponsible not to have more warm clothing and raincoats. While the lightning was dangerous, I believe it was the cold and wet that ultimately caused me to take shortcuts while rappelling.

Second, we should have begun descending the moment we saw signs of storms in the distance. A desire not to leave gear was part of the issue, and our desire to finish the trifecta of climbs we had started also probably led us to make a bad decision. The fear of lightning then led me to rush the rappel setups. Given all the tangles and the stuck rope, I don't believe rushing this way saved us any time at all.

Finally, and this is a minor point, a rope with a midpoint marker makes it a lot easier to set up a good rappel. (*Source: Anonymous report from the climber, male, age 29.*)

ROCKFALL, ANCHOR FAILURE | Overcrowding, Inexperience
Yosemite National Park, Cathedral Peak

On Friday, August 25, five climbers left the Bay Area with the goal of climbing Cathedral Peak. The team consisted of two experienced climbers (Ben and Nate) and three with little to no experience outside of the gym (Megan, Erin, and Andrew). All climbers were in their mid-20s.

Ben and Nate each had seven to ten years of climbing experience. Furthermore, they had gone to a self-rescue course together a year or so prior, and both had climbed Cathedral Peak numerous times.

On Saturday, August 26, the group arrived at the base of Cathedral Peak around 11:30 a.m. The southeast buttress is a very popular 5.6 climb, and this day was extremely busy, with an estimated 30–40 people on the route and at the base, including approximately 10 parties on variations of the first two pitches alone.

Due to the number of people on the "standard" start (route "A" in the popular Supertopo guidebook), the team decided to move right and start up what they believed to be route C. (During the investigation, it turned out they were closer to route B.) At around 12:45, they began climbing in two separate teams: Ben, Erin, and Megan, climbing with two ropes, and Nate and Andrew, climbing with one rope. Ben started leading on the left (staying fairly true to the "B route"), while Nate headed up a ways to the right. Both leaders soon got to the first ledge system, set up anchors, and began bringing up their partners.

Ben started belaying Erin first, and once she was a ways up the pitch, he began bringing Megan up on the other rope. Nate had already brought Andrew up to the first belay ledge and was getting ready to begin leading pitch two.

At about 1:15 p.m., Megan reached a point about 30 feet off of the ground, just as Erin was arriving at the belay ledge. After manteling onto the left side of the ledge, Erin put her foot on what appeared to be a solid rock and began to stand up. She felt the rock below her give way, and it fell toward Megan. Everyone who saw this began screaming, "ROCK! ROCK! ROCK!" to get Megan's attention. Megan saw the microwave-size block coming at her and moved to the right to get out of the way, but during its fall the rock hit something and changed its trajectory, causing it to hit Megan directly on the head. The impact knocked Megan unconscious.

As soon as the accident happened, Ben decided it was of the utmost importance to gain access to Megan and try to get her to the ground. The best course of action seemed to be to get Erin the rest of way to the belay, leave her attached to the anchor through his ATC Guide device, and fix the rest of her rope to the ground. This would allow him to rappel to Megan. Since his ATC was being used to keep Erin (and Megan) attached to the wall, he rappelled using a Munter hitch. Ben stated that he mis-tied the knot a number of times due to the frantic nature of the situation.

Nate also prepared to rappel. Leaving Andrew attached to the anchor with a personal anchor system (PAS), Nate doubled over his 60-meter rope and began rappelling toward Megan using an extended ATC with a prusik autoblock. To reach her, Nate had to pendulum hard left. Neither he nor the rest of the team noticed that after swinging over to a different area of the wall, his rope no longer reached the ground, due to the sharp elevation change along the base of the cliff. This will be important later in the narrative.

At the time of the accident, another team consisting of Patrick (male, 40s) and his partner had reached the base of the climb. After witnessing the event, Patrick asked his partner to belay him up to Megan. When he arrived at the scene, Patrick requested that Nate put in some gear for him. Nate placed a number 1 and number 2 Camalot, and Patrick clipped in to this temporary anchor with a PAS.

Meanwhile, Jenny, an emergency room doctor who also had started up the

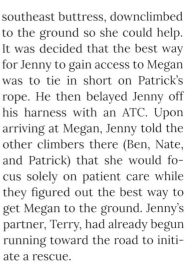

southeast buttress, downclimbed to the ground so she could help. It was decided that the best way for Jenny to gain access to Megan was to tie in short on Patrick's rope. He then belayed Jenny off his harness with an ATC. Upon arriving at Megan, Jenny told the other climbers there (Ben, Nate, and Patrick) that she would focus solely on patient care while they figured out the best way to get Megan to the ground. Jenny's partner, Terry, had already begun running toward the road to initiate a rescue.

With everyone on scene, the initial plan was to have Nate rappel with Megan using a "deadman rappel" (or rescue spider) on Nate's rope. The team began transferring Megan to Nate, clipping her PAS to a point on Nate's PAS, so Nate could rappel without having all of Megan's weight on his harness. The team also created a chest harness out of a shoulder sling to help keep Megan upright. Once they had checked to make sure she was securely attached, Patrick cut the taut rope leading from Megan's harness to Ben's original anchor above, thus committing Megan to Nate.

As Nate got ready, he suddenly realized that his rappel ropes did not reach the ground. Frustrated by this chain of events, the team realized they needed a new plan. Using a sling, Nate clipped himself directly into the two pieces he had placed for Patrick.

Since Jenny was still belayed on Patrick's ATC, the team's new plan was for Patrick to lower Jenny to the ground with Megan attached to her. To do this, the team clipped Megan directly to Jenny's harness using a Dyneema runner girthhitched through Megan's harness and attached to Jenny with two non-locking biners. In order to slowly transfer the load onto Jenny, Nate began rappelling a bit with Megan still attached to him.

[Top] Cathedral Peak, showing the approximate starts of routes A and B and the accident scene on the southeast buttress. (1) Rockfall origin. (2) Ben and Erin's belay anchor. (3) Nate and Andrew's belay anchor. (4) Rockfall impact. [Bottom] Origin of the rockfall at belay ledge is circled. Other loose blocks can be seen on the ledge. *NPS Photos*

During this process (about a six-inch lower), the two-piece "anchor," which previously had been unweighted, came under tension. The block where the anchor was built then shifted, and both cams pulled out. Fortunately, due to the interconnected nature of the scene, the anchor failure was not catastrophic. The whole team dropped about a foot, and then all five people were held by Nate's rappel rope.

After the drop, the team continued with the plan of lowering Jenny and Megan. Patrick climbed above the team and built a solid anchor with four cams. Once this was in place, Patrick redirected his rope through the new anchor and lowered the two women. Ben continued rappelling on his rope below Megan, supporting her during the lower. All told, the process of getting Megan to the ground after the rockfall took around 30 to 45 minutes.

At this point, it was around 2 p.m. Terry, Jenny's partner, had made contact with rangers in Tuolumne and initiated a rescue. A ground team and helicopter both were dispatched to the scene. At 3:17 pm, as the helicopter was doing a recon over the accident site, it was noticed that CPR on the patient was beginning. The ground team arrived on scene at approximately this time.

At 3:53 pm, after regaining pulses in the patient, she was short-hauled to a nearby landing zone, where she was then loaded into the helicopter and flown to Crane Flat. She was transferred to a medical helicopter and flown to Modesto Memorial Hospital. Unfortunately, she passed away in the emergency room.

ANALYSIS

While a climb like Cathedral Peak is not particularly difficult, move for move, it is every bit as serious as any other alpine rock climb. Loose rock abounds in the High Sierra, and it's important to test holds and be aware of your surroundings and climbers above and below you at all times.

While it's hard to know if—or to what extent—crowding on the route contributed to this accident, crowds are a common and dangerous problem on trade routes like Cathedral Peak. In addition to increased rockfall hazard, people's risk analysis, route choices, and the length of time on route can all be affected by having too many people in a small area. If there are too many people, consider another objective or waiting for another day.

The leaders of the party had knowledge of self-rescue systems (which helped tremendously), but they also struggled a bit when it came time to execute them. The amount of chaos and adrenaline in a scenario like this is tremendous. Without knowledge and practice, it will be extremely difficult to get things done efficiently. (In this case, the most efficient way to lower the patient likely would have been for Ben to anchor Erin at the belay ledge, release the autoblocked belay device—with a backup—and lower Megan directly to the ground. But the two leaders in the group were focused on reaching their injured friend as quickly as possible.

By acting hastily, the results can be catastrophic (such as the blown anchor) or simply add time and complexity to the rescue. Take a deep breath and analyze your surroundings. Ask yourself, "What is necessary? Who is necessary? What is our goal?" Remember: "Slow is smooth, smooth is fast." (*Source: Yosemite National Park Climbing Rangers.*)

LOWERING ERROR | Inexperience
Mammoth Lakes, Clark Canyon, Area 13

On July 25, as he was preparing to lower from a ledge, a climber fell about 15 meters to the ground. The climber was a member of a three-person team attempting a "mock multi-pitch climb" in preparation for a real multi-pitch objective later in the week. Climber 1 (male, age unknown, with moderate experience) conducted this practice session with Climber 2 (male, age 32) and Climber 3 (female, age 40). Both Climber 2 and Climber 3 had little outdoor climbing experience.

Before the fall, Climber 1 led up a climb (believed to be Chop Chop, 5.8) to a single bolt at a ledge approximately 15 meters up. He used this bolt as a belay anchor to bring up the other climbers. Before climbing, Climber 2 tied into the middle of the rope using a figure 8 on a bight clipped to his harness with a locking carabiner, and Climber 3 tied into the end of the rope.

Climber 2, still clipped into the rope via a figure 8 on a bight, attempted to lead the bolted climb above the ledge (Pachuco, 5.8) as the second pitch of their route. He was able to climb to the next bolt but felt "sketched out" and asked to be lowered to the ledge. Once there, Climber 2 asked to be lowered to the ground. Climber 2 recalled that, "the rope was a mess, with loops everywhere."

Concerned that he wouldn't have enough rope to lower Climber 2 from the bolt clipped on the route above, Climber 1 attached a second belay device to his harness, then redirected what he believed to be a length of rope leading to Climbing 2's knot through the anchor. Just as Climber 2 leaned back, Climber 1 realized that he was belaying "just a random loop" and Climber 2 fell to the ground.

Nearby climbers with medical experience and an AMGA-certified guide heard the scream of Climber 2 and came to assist. They stabilized Climber 2, who had a suspected spine injury and right forearm fracture, and called 911. Climber 1 and Climber 3 were shaken by the fall and were unable to self-rescue. The guide, belayed by another climber, ascended to their position and assisted them to the ground. Climber 1 sustained moderate rope burns to the inside of one hand, while Climber 3 sustained partial- and full-thickness rope burns exposing the "fatty" layer across her forearms and biceps. (*Source: RL, climber who assisted in the rescue.*)

ANALYSIS

Climber 1 said after the accident that this was the first time he had used the mock multi-pitch method of teaching and he was "coming up with most of it on the fly." He remarked that it quickly became "way too complicated."

When climbers are standing on a ledge, as in this instance, it can be difficult to identify the correct strands of rope to use for belaying, rappelling, or lowering, as none of them may be weighted. This makes the fundamentals of such transitions all the more essential. Climbers should be secured to an anchor prior to transitioning to another rope, and then should weight-test the rappel or lowering system before unclipping from the anchor. See Molly Loomis' Essentials article on this subject in Accidents 2017. (*Sources: the Editors and RL, a climber who assisted in the rescue.*)

GROUND FALL | Fixed Quickdraws Broke
Owens River Gorge

Jordan Cannon, 22, was attempting Bongo Fury (5.12b), a bolted arête in the Joe's Garage area, in late March. All of the bolts were pre-equipped with quickdraws made with thin Dynex (polyethylene) webbing. When Cannon fell above the third bolt, the quickdraws at both the third and second bolts broke and Cannon fell about 20 feet to the rocks below the route. He landed on his tailbone and hit his head on a rock but fortunately was not seriously hurt.

ANALYSIS

The hazards of fixed quickdraws are well-established. These quickdraws had been in place for about a year. The webbing on one of them broke at the upper carabiner (bolt end) and the other at the rope end. This climb receives little to no sun, but wind in the gorge likely caused the quickdraws to swing back and forth, abrading the webbing. Cannon said he did not see any damage to the draws, but the abrasion could have been hidden on the inside of the webbing. Fixed quickdraws of all kinds (including steel "perma-draws") also may develop worn grooves or burrs in the rope-end carabiner, which can shred or even cut a rope.

Fixed draws are convenient—and may be unavoidable on some climbs—but climbers should try to inspect them before attempting a route and consider replacing or supplementing them with their

Jordan Cannon holds the remnants of two quickdraws that broke when he fell past them in the Owens River Gorge. *Frank Dolan*

own quickdraws. Cannon was lucky to avoid more serious injury—this is a good example of the value of wearing helmets even on "well-protected" sport climbs. (Sources: *Jordan Cannon's Facebook posts and the Editors.*)

ANCHOR FAILURE | Inadequate Communication and Teamwork
High Sierra, Palisades, Starlight Peak

On August 6, a party of two was descending from Starlight Peak (14,200 feet) after climbing the Starlight Buttress route. Both climbers were experienced but unfamiliar with this particular area. They had planned to descend the northwest ridge to the Underhill Couloir between Starlight and Thunderbolt Peaks and then to the glacier.

While descending, the party deviated from their planned route. Climber 1 (male, 66) believed he had located a gully that could be scrambled down after an initial steep section, and requested that Climber 2 (female, 45) set up a rappel to start

Starlight Peak (center). The normal descent follows the right skyline to the snow couloir. The attempted shortcut headed down the steep sunlit face. *Jeff Mekolites*

down this gully. As Climber 1 rappelled into the gully, Climber 2 continued to assess the proposed route and concluded that leaving the ridge was a major mistake. She yelled to Climber 1 to stop and return, but he did not hear or respond. Climber 2 then rappelled down to Climber 1 and an argument occurred, with Climber 2 attempting to persuade Climber 1 to prusik back up the rope and continue down the ridge, while Climber 1 adamantly refused to consider this option. The party then pulled the rope, committing to the unknown descent.

The climbers completed several rappels down the gully before falling rock and difficulty constructing anchors caused them to leave the gully and begin rappelling diagonally across the neighboring face, leaving gear and natural (sling) anchors. Although they were unaware of it, the climbers were rappelling just right of the climb known as "the X." The Secor guidebook to the Sierra says, "This is probably the most dangerous route in the Palisades," because of loose rock.

Sometime in late afternoon, Climber 2 set a rappel anchor on the face, slinging a horn with webbing, and began rappelling. When Climber 2 was about 30 to 40 feet down the rappel, the anchor failed and both climbers fell, coming to a stop when the rope snagged on an unknown feature. Climber 1 was killed in the fall. Climber 2, who was not seriously injured, was crouched on a small ledge, tangled in the rope, with Climber 1 hanging below. Climber 2 managed to access an emergency locator beacon in her pack and activated it at this time.

Climber 2 had minimal gear available, as the majority was with her partner. She was unable to anchor herself and initially unwilling to move, due to the risk of being dragged off the ledge by the weight of Climber 1. After assessing the situation, she decided her position was too unstable to spend the night there without slipping and potentially dislodging the rope. She determined there were two load-bearing lengths keeping the rope tight: one tangled around her leg, pulling upward behind her to the unknown snag, and the other going downward from her jammed rappel device to Climber 1 hanging below. The strategy she implemented was to cut a long cord in two and use the two halves to attach a prusik knot to each of the load-bearing lengths of rope, connecting them loosely with a sling. She then carefully slid the prusik knot on the lower rope downward until she could transfer Climber 1's weight onto the prusik tied to the snagged rope. She was then able to remove herself from the weighted system, remove the jammed rappel device from the rope, and untangle herself from the remaining strands of rope.

Climber 2 climbed up to a larger ledge, about 20 feet above, where she tied herself to a boulder and remained through the night. Early the following morning (August 7), Climber 2 used the strobe on her emergency locator beacon to signal a guide and clients when they awoke at their nearby camp, and this party made their way across the glacier to where they could communicate. The guide called 911.

Helicopters from Sequoia and Kings Canyon National Parks and California Highway Patrol located Climber 2 but were unable to rescue her that afternoon. Inyo County Search and Rescue determined the area was too dangerous to access by climbing or rappel and requested assistance from Yosemite Search and Rescue. A YOSAR team arrived that evening by helicopter and rescued Climber 2 via a long line, after she'd spent 26 hours on the ledge. The YOSAR helicopter returned on August 8 to retrieve the body of Climber 1.

ANALYSIS

The immediate cause of this accident was that the final anchor set by Climber 2 failed. The difficulty of finding anchors, the lateness of the day, and the shortage of gear available for the descent led the party to rely on a natural anchor on unknown terrain, without a backup. Although it appeared solid and was tested before starting the rappel, it is likely the horn was not solidly attached to the rock. It is also possible the failure was due to other reasons, such as incorrectly tied webbing.

While the anchor failure was the immediate cause, the disagreement and decision to leave the standard route precipitated the event. Both parties should have assessed and discussed the proposed deviation from the standard descent before either climber began rappelling. (*Source: Anonymous report from Climber 2.*)

LEADER FALL | Inexperience, Inadequate Belay
Santa Monica Mountains, Echo Cliff

On December 3, my climbing partners Dave and Sam and a newly introduced third partner, Johnny, met up at Echo Cliffs and hiked to the crag called Easy Street. We split into teams of two, setting up ropes alongside each other. Dave and I began on Charlie Hustle (5.10a), while Sam and Johnny climbed Casey at the Bat (5.10b). Dave, a much stronger and more experienced climber than me, led our pitch. We were in direct sun and were all quickly drenched in sweat.

I successfully top-roped the route, feeling good and strong, and we decided to switch routes with Johnny and Sam. "You should lead this one, Sarah. I think you'd really like it," Sam told me as we transitioned. I hesitated, but my ego cushioned my nerves and I agreed to lead. Though I had been introduced to climbing as a child, I had just started to get serious about climbing four months prior to this trip. I had led a number of sport routes but had never taken a lead fall.

As I began the route, clipping the first three bolts, I began to feel more confident. At the third bolt, on a roof, I moved right using a ledge below. I took my time to feel for the best holds and calculate my moves over the roof. Dave had given me some slack, and I noticed that there was too much out, considering the ledge below. I felt inclined to voice this concern, but at that moment someone passed by and caught Dave's attention. Instead of interjecting for the sake of my safety and success, I decided to make the move. I reached with my left hand onto a positive but greasy hold, and as my weight transferred onto it I fell. The slack in the rope from the traverse and excess down at the belay resulted in a fall of 10 to 12 feet, past the ledge and onto an outwardly curved rock just below. My right foot took the complete force of the fall.

With the help of my partners, who piggybacked me much of the way, we made it back to the parking lot. The next day, I was diagnosed with a fractured right talus that required surgery, leaving me with a five-inch incision, two screws, and one plate to stabilize the fractured pieces of my ankle.

ANALYSIS

As a novice leader, I was naive when it came to observing fall lines, the risks involved in roofs and ledges, and the effects of the warmer weather. I was also insecure when it came to voicing my concerns to my belay partner when it was crucial to do so. Plus, my belayer was distracted during a crucial part of my climb. The belayer should always be "with me," with eyes focused on my climb and assessing risk from his/her viewpoint. In addition, none of us had a first-aid kit. A helpful climber offered me some anti-inflammatory medicine before we hiked out, but having NSAIDs of our own and splinting supplies would have been helpful. (*Source: Sarah Trudeau.*)

Editor's note: Falling is a part of sport climbing and is a learned skill. Though it might not have prevented this injury, practicing short leader falls in a safe environment (such as a gym), with an experienced mentor, can help novice climbers learn to take relaxed falls with feet and legs prepared to absorb impacts.

JOSHUA TREE SUMMARY | Call for Volunteers
Joshua Tree National Park

One fatal climbing accident was reported in Joshua Tree in 2017: Samuel Boldissar, 25, died as a result of head injuries after a ground fall from Spaghetti and Chili (5.7+) on Cyclops Rock. The precise cause of the fall is not known.

Two serious injuries occurred on Spiderman (5.10) in Conan's Corridor, including a leader (male, 26) who flipped upside down in a fall and suffered a very serious head injury (despite wearing a helmet) and a belayer whose femur was broken when a leader fall pulled the belayer off a rock and into a hole. Also notable: Two boulderers suffered tibia/fibula fractures as a result of falls.

Although there undoubtedly were many other, unreported climbing accidents in Joshua Tree during the year, official information is very limited from this park, and we rely on volunteers to submit first-person reports. Knowledgeable local climbers or first responders who would be interested in regularly contributing educational accident reports to this publication from Joshua Tree and other Southern California climbing areas are encouraged to write to us at accidents@americanalpineclub.org.

TAHQUITZ ROCK FATALITIES: *On July 8, a 51-year-old male climber's body was found at the base of the Trough (4 pitches, 5.4); it is not known whether he was soloing or scrambling to reach another route when he fell. On September 6, a climber (male, age 24) was killed and his brother seriously injured by rockfall in the Larks area on Tahquitz's north face. A warning about a large, loose boulder at the top of the exit gully for the Larks had been posted at Mountain Project two weeks before the accident.*

COLORADO

LEDGE FALL | Off-Route, Inadequate Protection
Estes Park Area, The Crags, Sharksfin

On August 20, Anders Fridberg and I (both very experienced) were climbing Blood in the Water, a three-pitch route on the north face of Sharksfin, south of Estes Park. Little did we realize the route's name would have some additional significance that day.

Anders led the second, crux pitch, which is gear-protected and 5.10+. The pitch is divided into two sections by a broad ledge. Above the ledge, the correct path is to clip a bolt and then ascend a stemming corner immediately above it. This corner looks hard to protect from below, but numerous gear placements soon appear.

Instead, after clipping the bolt, Anders traversed straight right on the ledge for about ten feet. He then started climbing what he thought was the correct line. He placed a number 3 Camalot about seven feet above the

Rescuers conduct a technical lower down steep talus toward a helicopter landing zone. *David Turner*

ledge, climbed an unknown distance past this piece, and then fell onto the ledge. Why and how far he fell is unknown, because Anders can't remember the fall. I could not see him from below.

Anders was unconscious for approximately one minute. Fortunately, he regained consciousness and was responsive. This helped greatly, as he was able to maneuver himself to the edge of the ledge so I could lower him to the belay atop the first pitch, and from there, pull the rope, rethread it, and lower him to the ground. It is also fortunate that Anders is a big, tough Swede because his injuries were horrific: a compound dislocation of his ankle, in which his lower leg bones broke through the skin.

Fortune smiled on the unfortunate yet again because we had cell phone service. We were just outside Rocky Mountain National Park, and the first responders to arrive were from the Park Service, about 2.5 hours after our call. Soon thereafter, volunteers from Rocky Mountain Rescue Group and Larimer County Search and Rescue reached us. A helicopter rescue was needed to evacuate Anders. (This crag is about an hour from the parking area on unimproved climbers' trails and steep talus.) An Army Blackhawk was flown in from Eagle, Colorado, and about 6.5 hours after our call for help, Anders was flown to a waiting ambulance in Estes Park.

ANALYSIS

With approximately 80 feet of rope out, there was too much stretch in the rope and too little protection, given the looming ledge below. I felt minimal force from the fall at the belay. Would a higher piece have prevented this accident, and if so, how much higher? Could a higher piece even have been placed? All good questions that Anders cannot answer. [*Editor's note: The only guidebook to this area was published before this route was established. The route is on Mountain Project, but the description of the climbing above the ledge is vague.*] We were fortunate to have a phone to call for help. In remote areas, where cell service might not be available, carrying a Spot or similar device should be considered. (*Source: David Turner.*)

ROCKY MOUNTAIN NATIONAL PARK SUMMARY: *Two people died in climbing-related accidents in 2017, and another was very seriously injured.*

On March 18, a 39-year-old man died, apparently while descending from the Loft, a high saddle at about 13,500 feet, after abandoning an attempt on Longs Peak. His two companions continued with their attempt, and, after discovering the man's vehicle still in the parking area that evening, they reported him missing. His body was found halfway up the Loft route, which often requires technical mountaineering in winter; the cause of death was not reported, but was likely a fall from snow or ice.

On September 30, a 66-year-old man died as a result of injuries from a fall reported to be 50 feet long at Batman Pinnacle on Lumpy Ridge. The climber was on Batman and Robin (5.6), whose first pitch does not follow an obvious well-protected line and has been the scene of a number of accidents.

At the end of October, a 31-year-old woman suffered life-threatening injuries from rockfall on Martha, a moderate mixed couloir on the south face of Mt. Lady Washington. She was lowered several hundred feet to the bottom of the climb and then down talus to a point where she could be hoisted into a helicopter. Martha is a very popular route, with both natural rockfall hazard and danger from other climbers; it generally has better snow and ice coverage later in the season.

In another incident, a 28-year-old man was injured in a ledge fall 700 feet up the Petit Grepon in August; climbers and rangers lowered him to the base of the spire, where he received advanced care from a park paramedic. The climber spent the night there with rescuers and then was lowered down 1,000 feet of talus to Sky Pond, where he could board a rescue helicopter. (*Sources: Rocky Mountain National Park and the Editors.*)

LOWERING ERROR | Belayer Pulled Into Rock, No Helmet
Boulder Canyon, Cascade Crag

On September 13, a belayer began lowering a climber from a sport route with an ATC Guide device. The climber outweighed the belayer by roughly 50 percent. The belayer, standing on unstable rocky ground about six to eight feet away from the wall, was pulled off balance during the lower. She spun to the left and fell toward the rock face, hitting her head and left side. However, the belayer was able to hold onto the brake strand, keeping the climber from falling very far. Another climber quickly came to assist and finished lowering the climber, using the belayer's device. The belayer, whose injuries included a head laceration and cracked ribs, was evacuated to the nearby road.

ANALYSIS

The belayer was located too far from the wall on unstable terrain and wasn't anchored (to a tree, a ground anchor, or other solid anchor), a useful practice when the climber significantly outweighs the belayer. This incident is also a good reminder of the importance of wearing a helmet (and good shoes) while belaying single-pitch climbs from the ground. To the belayer's credit, she managed to maintain her grip on the brake strand despite the impact and her injuries. (*Source: Anonymous report from the climber.*)

FALL ON ROCK | Communication Error, Taken Off Belay
Boulder Canyon, The Dome

On August 5, I and another emergency physician witnessed a horrific fall from the Dome. We were scouting locations for an upcoming practice session, as we both volunteer for Rocky Mountain Rescue Group. I saw the climber bounce several times, then fall out of sight. I called 911 to report an estimated 60- to 70-foot fall and let dispatch know a technical rescue would be needed.

When we reached the scene, the climber was suspended on his rope about three feet off the ground, unconscious and bloodied. A bystander cut the rope with a knife, and the injured climber was lowered by several people to the ground. The climber, age 27, regained consciousness after several minutes. He was loaded in a litter and carried

The Dome in Boulder Canyon. A climber fell from near the top to the approximate area marked by the arrow. *John Hegyes*

down the Dome approach trail, and was in an ambulance less than an hour after the accident occurred. He ended up with multiple injuries, including a concussion, wicked road rash, and some fractures, but no surgeries. I ran into him at a local pub (using crutches and with a neck brace) about a week later!

ANALYSIS

The climber, who had some experience, was with two beginners. He had climbed East of the Sun (5.7) and was planning to set up a top-rope on the East Slab using his single rope. After building an anchor, he leaned back to lower, but he had been taken off belay. The climber bounced down the entire slab until, miraculously, an overhand knot in the end of the rope caught in a carabiner clipped to his first piece of protection. I don't know if this knot was placed intentionally, but this piece, a wired nut about 30 feet off the deck, kept him from hitting the ground.

When talking with him later in the pub, the climber accepted responsibility for what had happened, as he was the most experienced one there. He did not remember the fall or the rescue. The party's inexperience resulted in a classic communication error: The climber was taken off belay before being lowered.

Before leaving the ground, the climber should always explain to the belayer his or her plan for when the pitch is completed (lower, rappel, bring up the next climber, etc.). The belayer must not take the climber off belay without audible or visual confirmation that the climber is anchored and off belay. (*Sources: Dr. Alison Sheets and the Editors.*)

MORE BOULDER CANYON ACCIDENTS: *In March, a woman was lowered off the end of her rope on Frothing Green at the Bowling Alley, suffering a head laceration in a tumbling fall. The pitch is obviously long and is best climbed with a 70-meter rope (some route descriptions warn of this), and a stopper knot in the belayer's end of the rope would have prevented this accident. At the end of May, a climber took a reported 50-foot fall at Tonnere Tower; fortunately, a tree broke his fall, but his injuries still necessitated a difficult evacuation. In June, a 29-year-old woman fell from the tricky-to-protect first pitch of Cosmosis (5.10a) at Bell Buttress; a nut and small cam pulled out, and she hit the belay ledge 20 to 25 feet below, breaking an ankle and possibly vertebrae.*

FALL ON ROCK | Failure to Clip Anchor
Eldorado Canyon, The Bastille

On May 12, 27-year-old Conor Felletter and his climbing partner, Kelly Kochanski, were climbing Werk Supp, a two-pitch 5.9 route. After completing the first pitch, Felletter decided to head over to the Bastille Crack, a popular five-pitch 5.7 that already had another party on it. He climbed an easy gully for 80 feet to join the fourth pitch of the Bastille Crack. Continuing up that pitch, Felletter passed the traditional belay stance, already occupied by the other party, and began to set up an anchor higher and to the left. He placed one solid cam but did not clip it right away, focusing instead on placing a second piece for his anchor. Before he could place the second piece, he slipped.

Felletter fell 40 feet, flipping upside down and hitting his head on a rock, which split his helmet and gashed his forehead. He was unresponsive at first but regained consciousness and motioned for Kochanski to lower him to a ledge. Another climber reached the ledge and helped Kochanski secure Felletter. This second climber also called 911. The patient stated that his neck hurt, and he was drifting in and out of consciousness.

Rocky Mountain Rescue Group (RMRG) responded within the hour, rappelling to the climbers' position from the top of the Bastille. After evaluating Felletter's injuries and stabilizing him, a lowering system was rigged. Felletter was secured in a litter and lowered to the ground and a waiting ambulance. He suffered seven broken vertebrae in his neck, three broken ribs, a torn elbow ligament, many lacerations, and moderate brain trauma. He attributes being alive to his helmet and the quick response of the RMRG.

The place where Felletter attempted to set up his anchor was dirtier and wetter than the main route, and it is possible he slipped on loose debris. Although some climbers like to complete an anchor before clipping in (perhaps waiting until they have a master point linked to all the anchor components), it requires no significant time or effort to temporarily clove-hitch the rope to your first solid anchor piece or clip your personal tether to it. Rescuers noted that Felletter's first piece was good and likely would have held his slip. (*Sources: Rocky Mountain Rescue Group, published accounts, and the Editors.*)

FOXTROT GROUND FALL: *In January a climber hit the ground when a key protection piece pulled out of Foxtrot (5.11d) on the West Ridge after a fall. The climber, who was not wearing a helmet, had a head laceration. A similar accident occurred the previous year on the same climb.*

Rocky Mountain Rescue evacuates a patient from the Bastille in Eldorado Canyon. *Alison Sheets*

GROUND FALL | Protection Pulled Out
Eldorado Canyon, Rincon Wall

On March 27, Japhy Dhungana (32), Eric Whewell, and Rainbow Weinstock were climbing at the Rincon Wall, projecting single-pitch trad-climbing routes. All three are very experienced climbers; each is an AMGA-certified rock guide. Each person had a separate project he was working in "headpoint" style. It was Japhy's second day attempting the Evictor (5.12d R), and he had practiced his gear placements and climbing beta, including successfully top-roping the route while "mock-placing" gear along the way. After five attempts that day, three of which were successful sends on top-rope, Japhy began a lead attempt late in the day, around 4 p.m.

Japhy started up the route with just the right gear on his harness. The lower one-third of this climb is considered the "safety crux," with sparse gear placements over challenging climbing, and this section was dispatched without trouble. At the halfway mark, there is one horizontal crack with a decent rest. At this horizontal crack, Japhy placed number 0.75 and 0.5 Black Diamond Ultralight Camalots adjacent to each other, equalized by a single quickdraw clipped to both of the cams. This horizontal crack offered the best protection on the whole route, and the two cams nested together created a "mini-anchor" that would help protect the upper climb.

Above this horizontal crack, the "redpoint crux" is a long sequence of sparsely protected 5.12 moves. In a shallow crack, Japhy placed a 0.4 Ultralight Camalot and a 0.75 Ultralight Camalot. Both placements were good, but due to the shallowness and shape of the crack, they were not very deep and the stems could not be oriented toward the direction of load (i.e., they were pointing outward from the vertical crack). Japhy climbed past the crux moves and reached for the finishing jug, where a bomber nut could be placed. At this point, he was about 10 feet above the last piece of protection (the 0.75 Camalot). He could not control the final jug and slipped off, expecting to take a 25- to 30-foot fall. Instead, he landed on the ground next to his belayer after a 70-foot ground fall. Four pieces of gear had ripped from their placements, and the belayer never felt the rope come under tension.

Although Japhy suffered significant injuries (fractured pelvis, fractured sacrum, fractured lumbar spine, concussion, and significant internal bleeding), he was soon able to return to climbing and working as a guide. His helmet likely protected him from a more serious head injury. He is grateful to all of the rescue personnel and is glad to be able to continue climbing with more humility and experience.

ANALYSIS

Upon significant reflection, it seems highly likely that the upper pieces pulled out after rotating in their shallow placements due to the strong downward force of a leader fall applied to the stiff stems of the cams. Japhy knew these the upper pieces were not 100 percent, which is why he had doubled up the pieces just below.

The real surprise in this incident is the failure of the two pieces of protection in the horizontal crack. These were in a deep crack in good rock. They were placed next to each other, well seated, and within a good camming range. They were so close to each other that they could be clipped with a single quickdraw. Yet both cams ripped—the rope did not come unclipped from the rope-end carabiner. Although this is speculation, it seems likely that the high force of the fall may have caused one of the two nested cams to knock the other one out of position, much like a bowling ball hitting pins. It is worth wondering: Would placing just one of these cams have been safer? It's also possible that the smooth rock inside this climb's cracks may have affected the cams' holding power.

Another speculative possibility is that Ultralight Camalots, with their narrower cam lobes and slightly stiffer plastic housing, may not have been the right choice for this route. A camming unit with a more flexible stem, especially in the upper two placements, might have been less likely to pull out. A lesson here is that having a range of protection options, and not just relying on one style of cam, could help protect complex routes such as this, where precise gear beta is essential.

Finally, headpoint-style climbs like this are dangerous, and large lead falls on traditional gear can have unpredictable results. A more fastidious selection of camming devices appropriate to the route, not attempting to lead the route after a full day of climbing, and perhaps testing the critical gear placements before a lead attempt would all be good strategies for climbs like this. (*Source: Japhy Dhungana.*)

Editor's note: You can hear Japhy Dhungana tell this story in greater detail in episode 24 of the Sharp End Podcast.

FIRST FLATIRON FATALITIES: *Two male soloists died in separate falls from the popular First Flatiron above Boulder. In one case, deteriorating weather likely was a factor, as rain and snow moved in during the man's climb. The accessible, low-angle slabs of the Flatirons frequently lure inexperienced or ill-prepared scramblers (including those with inadequate footwear) into dangerous positions, forcing rescues.*

LOWERING ERROR | Rope Too Short

South Platte, Devils Head, Recovery Room

This accident occurred after a climber completed a long route (Sex Face, 5.12a) during which he linked two pitches from the ground. While descending from the top of the second pitch, the climber was lowered off the end of the rope, resulting in a ground fall of approximately 25 feet. The climber landed on his back on uneven rocks, resulting in significant injuries necessitating helicopter evacuation, hospitalization, and surgery. Injuries included abrasions, lacerations, fracture, spinal injury, internal injuries, hemopneumothorax, and subsequent pulmonary edema.

ANALYSIS

As is often the case, a series of "small" errors overlapped to cause a large accident.

Rope too short. The climber was told by multiple people that the two pitches of this climb could be linked and lowered using a 70-meter rope. The climber's rope originally had been 80 meters long but had been cut down. The climber believed his rope was still more than 70 meters long, but was incorrect. It was later measured at just over 55 meters.

Belay system not closed. The climber had tied a stopper knot in the end of the rope at the beginning of the day. However, while seconding the route just prior to the one where the accident occurred, the belayer untied the stopper knot in order to tie in to her harness. After completing that route, she pulled the rope and the stopper knot was not replaced. Neither party caught the error.

It also may have been a factor that the belayer climbed primarily indoors and was not in the habit of placing stopper knots or otherwise closing the system. As a climber, checking the stopper knot should be part of your pre-climb ritual, just as you would check your knot and make sure you're on belay. Use this habit indoors to ingrain it into your practice.

Belayer failed to keep track of the end of the rope, thus allowing it to pass through the belay device. Focus primarily on the end of the rope while lowering rather than the climber. Lower slowly. Tie the rope to the rope bag, which would provide an auditory and visual clue the rope end is near.

Distraction. During the lower-off, another person was talking to the climber and belayer. It's possible this small distraction contributed to the belayer and climber failing to notice the inadequate rope remaining.

Situational awareness. Racking more than 20 quickdraws and linking two pitches should have been red flags for the climber and belayer, reminding them that this long route would require extra care while lowering. (*Source: Anonymous report from the climber.*)

FATAL RAPPEL ERROR AT SHELF ROAD: *A 27-year-old man died after falling about 60 feet to the ground at the Bank sector of Shelf Road, near Cañon City. The climber had limited outdoor experience, and witnesses reported that he fell from the anchor atop a limestone sport climb after incorrectly threading or clipping his rappel device to descend.*

LONG FALL AND EPIC SELF-RESCUE
Elk Mountains, Pyramid Peak

In late morning on March 5, Ryan Montoya, 23, had nearly completed a solo winter ascent of 14,018-foot Pyramid Peak, near Aspen. After spending the night at the foot of the peak and climbing the west face and northwest ridge (4th class), he was about 40 feet from the top at 11 a.m., in clouds, light snowfall, and no wind. As he moved toward the summit, he either slipped on a loose rock or fell through a small cornice, and in an instant he started falling down the east face, a legendary extreme ski run. Montoya tumbled at least 1,500 vertical feet over snow and rocks before coming to a stop in soft snow.

Montoya's pelvis was broken in three places and an elbow was partially dislocated. His helmet was shattered. He was still at least 2,500 feet above the valley floor and miles away from any regularly traveled trail or road. He had lost one glove, his headlamp, and both of his ice axes, and he'd left his sleeping bag in a snow cave on the other side of the mountain. He still had a small stove and fuel, a shovel, a plastic emergency bivy sack, warm clothes, a few chemical hand warmers, and some food and water.

Ryan Montoya fell over 1,500 feet down the east side of Pyramid Peak, then self-evacuated for two and a half days despite severe injuries. *Ryan Montoya | Google Earth*

After the fall, worried about avalanches, he slid and scooted down the rest of the east face to the valley, where he was able to stock up on water and dig a shallow cave to spend the night. Snowfall and high winds (approaching 100 mph at the height of Pyramid's summit) kept him in the cave until midafternoon the next day. When he emerged, Montoya found he had less pain in his hip and decided to try to walk down the valley. He slowly made progress and that evening spent another night in a small cave. The next day he continued walking, eventually covering about four miles through snow.

Montoya had been reported missing the night of his fall, but searchers focused on the west side of the mountain, where he had started. They found his snow cave and skis and feared he might have been caught in an avalanche. In late afternoon, however, Montoya reached the closed Maroon Creek Road and ran into some backcountry travelers, who quickly alerted Mountain Rescue Aspen. He made it to the hospital that evening. In addition to his injuries from the fall, Montoya had frostbite on the fingers of one hand, where his remaining glove had gotten wet.

ANALYSIS

Though one could point to small errors of judgment that led up to Montoya's fall, his perseverance and aptitude after the accident were extraordinary. Montoya was an experienced, well-prepared, and remarkably tough mountaineer who largely self-rescued despite great adversity. He wrote a full account of this incident that can be found at 14ers.com. Also highly recommended is Montoya's interview with Ashley Saupe in episode 17 of the Sharp End Podcast, in which he describes the ordeal and the lessons learned in detail. (*Sources: Ryan Montoya, 14ers.com, published accounts, and the Editors.*)

FALL ON ROCK | Off-Route
Elk Mountains, Capitol Peak, Northwest Buttress

On July 23, a female climber (25, 15 years of experience) and her male climbing partner (24, six years of experience) were climbing the Northwest Buttress route (IV 5.9) on Capitol Peak. By simul-climbing most of the route, the pair was able to reduce the total pitches from 13 to eight.

On the seventh pitch, the climbers encountered a 5.7 roof with loose blocks, which they had expected based on photos and route beta. The female climber took the lead, moving up the low-angle face and placing a few pieces before the roof. She noticed a few small rocks being knocked off by the rope above her belayer, so she moved left in hopes that rockfall would not hit her partner. She placed a number 0.3 Camalot X4 and stepped up approximately five feet to reach the roof. As she made her first move onto the roof, some blocky rocks collapsed and she tumbled down along with head- to computer-size boulders.

The belay held, but the climber's right foot was pinned beneath some of the fallen rocks. She trundled the rocks off her foot and was able to stand on the slope. Her belayer lowered her to a flat spot and they taped up abrasions and lacerations on her fingers, arms, and face. Although in pain, she was able to continue climbing with the injured ankle. The pair finished the route and descended via the standard northeast ridge (Knife Edge) route, staying roped up for the fourth-class sections.

ANALYSIS
Capitol Peak is known for loose rock, even on the relatively solid Northwest Buttress. The leader may have climbed into an area of the roof that was less stable than the more frequently climbed section a few feet to the right. Instead of moving off-route, the team might have been able to relocate the belay or link pitches to protect the belayer from potential rockfall. However, they said, they were belaying from bolted anchors and had limited options. The climber knocked on the blocks in the roof prior to stepping up and said they seemed sufficiently stable. "Besides being super-cautious, I'm not sure how else the accident could have been avoided," she said. (*Source: Anonymous report from the climber.*)

CAPITOL PEAK FATALITIES | Off-Route, Inexperience
Elk Mountains

An unprecedented five fatalities occurred within a six-week span on 14,137-foot Capitol Peak, one of Colorado's most challenging 14ers. The mountain's standard route, the northeast ridge, is a 17-mile round trip concluding with an exposed

Capitol Peak's Northwest Buttress route (5.9) is in center. The normal route (the 4th-class Knife Edge) is near the left skyline. Several climbers have died attempting shortcuts down this very steep face.

stretch of 4th-class rock.

On July 15, Jake Lord (25) fell at least 160 feet between Daly Saddle and K2, a subsummit of Capitol. Lord and his climbing partner, Peter Doro, were not on the standard route but instead following a nearby ridge that is often taken in error. Lord was climbing over a large boulder when it came loose, causing him to fall. Doro climbed down to Lord, called emergency services, and began CPR. The patient was dead by the time Mountain Rescue Aspen (MRA) volunteers arrived at the scene about two hours after the call.

On August 6, Jeremy Shull (35) fell approximately 200 feet from the east side of the ridge between K2 and the Knife Edge, the 4th-class crux of the climb. Shull, an experienced climber, was with three friends, but he was ahead and out of sight when he fell. He fell into a "crevasse" and was confirmed dead later that day by an MRA volunteer. The recovery effort, postponed several days by bad weather, was extensive and dangerous due to the location of the body.

On August 22, the bodies of Aspen couple Carlin Brightwell (27) and Ryan Marcil (26) were found at the base of the northwest face of Capitol. They were last seen in late morning of August 20, very near the summit. It's not known what caused their fall, but according to Jesse Steindler, a deputy with the Pitkin County Sheriff's Office, the couple may have tried to descend an alternative route from the top.

On August 26, Zackaria White (21) fell approximately 600 feet while descending the mountain. White and his climbing partner, Brandon Wilhelm, had argued over which route to take down the mountain. White, with little previous climbing experience, wanted to try an apparent direct descent from the top down a gully to the north. Wilhelm, who had climbed 42 of Colorado's 14ers, advised against leaving the standard route and warned White that the shortcut would cliff out. The pair separated before the Knife Edge around 4:45 p.m., approximately an hour after reaching the summit, and White began to descend the gully. Wilhelm continued down the standard route and reached Capitol Lake around 7 p.m. He searched for White until he could no longer see in the darkness. White's body was found the next day.

ANALYSIS

Four fatalities had occurred on Capitol Peak over the preceding 14 years before the spike in 2017. Capitol Peak is not a beginner climb and should not be attempted unless the climber has extensive Class 4 mountaineering experience. Climbers should build their capability patiently, creating a solid foundation. Climbing peaks with an experienced mentor or hiring a guide service can help with skill development and understanding personal limitations.

As many as four out of the five climbers who died on Capitol in 2017 were off-route, demonstrating that an important step in preparation is to thoroughly research the planned ascent and descent. In addition to printed guidebooks, resources such as 14ers.com provide extensive route information, photos, and comments on route-finding and current conditions from fellow climbers. From the top of Capitol Peak, it appears there is a more direct route back to Capitol Lake, the start of the climb. According to Justin Hood, president of MRA, this descent becomes progressively steeper on loose talus and scree, ending with an unavoidable 300-foot cliff band. It can also be very difficult to return this way once climbers realize they cannot continue down.

Most climbers attempting Capitol do not bring harnesses, rope, and a rack. But with loose rock and high exposure, the consequences of a misstep are high. Knowledgeable climbers can safeguard the most exposed sections of this climb with a short rope and very little additional equipment (*see Know the Ropes on page 8*).

Along with appropriate experience and preparation, climbers must use good judgment. "Everyone is in charge of their own decisions," said MRA's Hood. "Oftentimes, there is an expectation that you have to summit, because you took the time off of work, got on the plane, rented the car, lugged the equipment and camped, and want the Instagram shot. If you can be in the moment and let go of your expectation to summit, you will make better, safer decisions."

To respond to the increase of mountaineering accidents in the region, the National Forest Service, MRA, and Pitkin County Sheriff's Office are organizing workshops to educate climbers on mountain safety. Partnering with Aspen Alpine Guides and Aspen Expeditions, they will focus on techniques that will help climbers navigate the unique hazards of the Elk Mountains. See mountainrescueaspen.org.

FALL FROM ANCHOR | Communication Problems
Durango Area, Lemon Reservoir

Thad Ferrell and I arrived at Lemon Reservoir in the upper Florida River Valley around 8 a.m. on September 9. It's about a 15-minute hike in, followed by a 20-foot downclimb into the canyon. We did three warm-up routes, all sport climbs. I led each of the routes first, followed by Thad. At the top of each route, he would clip in and give me a thumbs-up, and then set up a rappel and rap down. We used verbal commands, but we couldn't hear each other because of the river running by us.

We next headed over to a 5.12- called Holy Grail. We decided to wear helmets because there was a slight chance of hitting a ledge about two-thirds of the way up. I climbed first, putting up the draws. I fell at the crux and wanted to do the route again. However, just as Thad started climbing, two other climbers, George and Ian, told us they also wanted to do the route. We briefly discussed this, but as Thad started up we still hadn't determined if I was going to climb the route again. I remember thinking that I should remind Thad to leave the quickdraws in place on his way down. Saying something likely would have prevented the accident, because we both would have been on the same page about what was going to happen at the anchor.

Thad sent the route. Shortly thereafter, he gave me the thumbs-up and I took him off belay, the same steps we had followed on all three previous routes. Soon after this, he fell. I dove out of the way because Ian and George were yelling "rock!" Thad landed with a terrible thud. It was the worst moment of my life.

Ian and George immediately ran to him. Down the trail about 100 feet, a dozen or so climbers were across the river, and they shouted to me that they were going to run out and call for help. Someone else had a SPOT device and activated it immediately. Two other men, Chas and a second Ian, ran over to the scene. And then I collapsed and two women came across the river to sit with me.

Thad was unconscious for eight minutes. I thought he was dead. But one of the Ians came over to tell me he was breathing and likely didn't have a spinal injury. (George, the two Ians, and Chas all had Wilderness First Responder training.) Thad started moving fairly quickly after he regained consciousness, but was clearly in terrible shape. He was extremely disoriented. His helmet was broken.

Rescuers showed up within the hour, followed shortly by Flight for Life. They organized people to get him across the river and up to the helicopter. I left with Rosie to call Thad's wife.

Thad was flown to the local hospital and then to St. Anthony's in Denver, where he had a bunch of surgeries. He sustained numerous traumatic injuries, the most serious being a shattered jaw. The four first responders had saved his life by keeping his airway clear. Because he had no serious brain or spine injuries, Thad will recover almost fully. He was already walking a couple of months after the accident.

ANALYSIS

Despite both of us having 20-plus years of experience in all realms of climbing (trad, sport, bouldering, ice, alpine), we didn't clearly communicate about what Thad was going to do at the belay while we were on the ground. We were sport climbing and nonchalant about it. What went right:

(1) WFR-trained people were there within seconds of the fall.

(2) Someone across the river had a SPOT device and could call for help almost immediately.

(3) We wore helmets.

(4) Thad is a mutant.

When he gave me the thumbs-up at the anchor, I thought he was off belay and planned to rappel, just as he had earlier. He does not remember anything about the accident. I surmise that he was thinking he was going to leave the quickdraws on the route for George and Ian and simply lower off the draws I had left at the anchor. He was still tied into his end of the rope, and the rope fell to the ground with him.

My WFR certification had expired 20 years earlier, so I wasn't equipped to help Thad after the fall, except to take notes on his vitals. Had the four first responders not been there, I am not sure he would have survived.

I feel extreme guilt for not being able to help and for taking him off belay. It doesn't matter how many people tell me it was an accident or that it wasn't my fault. I feel responsible, at least in part. I don't know how people deal with stuff like this without seeing a trauma therapist. (*Source: Lizzy Scully.*)

KENTUCKY

BELAYER PULLED INTO WALL | Miscommunication
Red River Gorge, Miller Fork Nature Preserve, Fruit Wall

On April 29, a 25-year-old male was belaying a 22-year-old male climber on JewJew Fruit (5.10c) at Fruit Wall. The climber, who was attempting to flash the route, had progressed to just below the seventh bolt. He clipped a quickdraw to the bolt and pulled up slack a number of times in an attempt to clip the rope, but each time dropped it. The belayer could tell he was getting close to the failure point.

With the rope in his hand, the leader yelled "take!" and the belayer, hoping the leader had managed to clip the seventh bolt, took in an arm's length of slack and then saw a "bunch" more rope fall toward him. The belayer moved backward, about 10 feet away from the cliff, without the rope coming taut. At this point the climber (who, in fact, had not clipped the seventh bolt) fell off and pulled the belayer rapidly into the wall, fracturing his right calcaneus (heel).

ANALYSIS
While the leader and belayer had climbed together, they were not regular partners. The belayer later said that none of his regular partners would have yelled "take" when he was still trying to clip the next bolt and was well above the previous bolt. Initially, the belayer said, he had been stationed close to the wall with a "slight J" of slack in the rope leading from his Petzl Grigri 2 to the climber, but he moved backward in an attempt to take up the surprising amount of slack when the leader asked him to "take." The climber also outweighed the belayer by 35-40 pounds, and this likely contributed to the severity of the pull. (*Sources: The belayer, belayer's Mountain Project post, and the Editors.*)

GROUND FALL | Inadequate Belay, No Helmet
Red River Gorge, Roadside Crag

Early in the afternoon on August 27, EJ and LS (both age 21) were climbing Trouble Clef (5.9), an 80-foot sport route, when EJ took a lead fall above the last protection bolt as he neared the anchors. LS, who was belaying with a tube-style device, failed to arrest the fall. The resulting ground fall of approximately 70 feet caused abrasions, lacerations, and concussion/head trauma. It was LS's first time belaying, and a backup belayer was not employed. Wolfe County Search and Rescue performed a carry-out to waiting paramedics, and the subject was transported via helicopter to University of Kentucky Trauma Hospital, where he was treated for head injuries. The climber was not wearing a helmet.

ANALYSIS
The climber weighed 195 pounds and the belayer about 115 pounds—a difference of approximately 80 pounds. This resulted in the belayer getting pulled up the cliff face when the climber fell. It is likely that this jolt and the belayer's impact with the

cliff caused this inexperienced belayer to lose control of the brake strand.

As a general rule, belayers should stand directly underneath the first piece of protection to minimize the distance he or she is pulled up and across the ground while arresting a fall. A ground anchor or ballast also could have been used. Perhaps most important, given this belayer's inexperience, a backup belayer should have been employed.

The Edelrid Ohm can help small belayers catch much heavier climbing partners.

Two types of belay technology can help a belayer who is much lighter than the climber. The Edelrid Ohm, a device that is clipped to the first bolt of a sport climb or gym climb, is specifically designed to mitigate the effects of weight disparities between climbers and belayers. In addition, an assisted braking belay device might have prevented loss of control by the belayer. (*Source: Wolfe County Search and Rescue.*)

BELAYER ERROR AND GROUND FALL AT ROADSIDE CRAG: *In early June, a climber took a 35-foot ground fall from the fifth bolt on Fadda (5.10a sport) due to belayer error. While the climber's fall was partially arrested by his belayer, slowing his descent, he struck the ground at a high rate of speed, resulting in multiple abrasions and traumatic injuries to his ribs and pelvis. (Source: Wolfe County Search and Rescue.)*

MICHIGAN

FALL ON ICE | Transition Error, Inexperience
Upper Peninsula, Munising

On February 17, during the Michigan Ice Fest, a woman and two men, all in their 20s, set out to climb the steep pillar of Strawberry Daze (WI4), approaching from the top. The men had climbed ice before but the woman, who borrowed ice climbing equipment from the festival, was a beginner.

Planning to top-rope, they rappelled about 25 meters down to a belay behind the pillar, where an icy ledge had formed high above the shore of Lake Superior. The woman was unable to complete the climb. Partway up, she decided it would be easier to ascend the climbing rope. She was carrying ascenders and successfully transitioned to ascending but was unable to make it to the top. Deciding to try climbing again, she began to transition back to a rappel to return to the ledge. During this transition, she fell about seven meters and landed on the belay ledge. She complained of substantial pain in her pelvis (which turned out to be bruised but not fractured).

The trio attempted to self-rescue from the top but were unable to get her out.

It was a warm day (about 30°F), but they were starting to get cold. They had radios and called 911. The Coast Guard flew out a helicopter and put a rescuer onto the 45° ice slope at the base of the cliff, but the rescuer did not have crampons and was unable to climb the ice to the belay ledge.

Ice Fest leaders then organized a team of four professional climbers and guides to assist with the rescue. It was now pitch dark. The climbers were transported by tracked vehicle and snowmobile, and then went on foot to the scene. After rappelling to the belay ledge, the climbing rescuers were able to lower the woman about 25 meters to the icy shore. The Coast Guard flew the helicopter back with their rescue swimmer, who was able to get the injured climber into a scoop basket so she could be lifted out. All of the climbers were back at the trailhead by around 3:30 am.

ANALYSIS

Depending on the season, Strawberry Daze (rated WI4) can have very difficult

Coast Guard rescue swimmer awaits a helicopter during a late-night mission. above Lake Superior.
Karsten Delap

sections, and the approach from above is somewhat committing. A climb that can be accessed from the bottom, where retreat is simple, would be a more appropriate choice for a new ice climber.

Backup knots or hitches should always be used when ascending or making any sort of transition in the safety system. Had the climber tied a backup hitch to the rappel rope before attempting to load her device, she probably would not have fallen.

In places where there is no established mountain rescue team, rescues may take substantially longer. Choose an appropriate adventure based on experience of the party, available equipment, and weather conditions. (*Source: Karsten Delap.*)

NEVADA

GROUND FALL | Inadequate Protection
Nevada, Red Rock National Conservation Area, Calico Basin

Paul and I had been climbing at Red Rock for about a week. I am very familiar with Red Rock Canyon, having climbed there for a few weeks a year since 2014, when I took the American Alpine Institute (AAI) courses "Intensive Intro to Rock Climbing" and "Learn To Lead."

On February 7, we headed to the Red Spring area, started with a few routes on Cowlick Crag, then headed over to Dickies Cliff. The route we chose was Guys and Ghouls (100', 5.6), which I had top-roped during one of the AAI courses. Because of my injuries, I don't recall the details of the climb and fall. Here is what I have put together based on discussions with witnesses.

I started leading up the route and put in a small cam (approximately 0.4 Camalot) about 15 feet off the deck. I pulled a small roof and continued up 10 to 12 feet above my cam. At this point I fell. I don't know why, and neither do the people who saw the fall. No one saw a hold break.

Initially, Paul caught my fall. But then some bad things happened. First, the force of the catch (I dropped over 20 feet) and the sudden and forceful upward pull of the harness on my skin caused a bad subcutaneous degloving injury to my backside (specifically a Morel-Lavallée lesion of the posterior iliac region).

Second, the micro-cam at 15 feet, after initially holding a force powerful enough to seriously injure me, pulled out. I dropped the remaining five or six feet to the base of the climb, then bounced another 10 feet below that into a rocky gully. My head impacted the rock several times, causing skull fractures and a traumatic brain injury.

A wilderness first responder named Jason saw the fall and came running to help. Jason described me as "unconscious and unresponsive," with bleeding from the nose and ears. He and Paul called for a rescue and watched over me until a helicopter came and the EMTs took me to the hospital.

ANALYSIS

I was on a route I had climbed three years earlier, and I am certain it was well within my ability. I will never understand how I could have fallen where I did, but sometimes climbers fall. (Maybe I stepped on a banana peel!) I would say the biggest takeaway is the adage, "Always have at least two pieces between you and the ground."

Some people have mentioned the possibility of the belayer employing a "soft catch" as something that might have prevented the cam from pulling. But my conclusion is that my belayer made the correct choice in this situation. Given the distance I had climbed above the cam, a ground fall was definitely a possible outcome, and the belayer's primary concern is to keep the climber from hitting the ground.

Although it had rained a tiny bit two or three days before the accident, I don't believe this had any impact on the rock quality or the cam placement. It was a fairly small Camalot, so maybe this was a case of over-reliance on a small cam. I would point out, in my defense, that the piece held temporarily with enough force to give me a nasty injury, so it wasn't a completely useless placement.

I'm sure that wearing a helmet is among the reasons I survived the fall. I recommend it. (*Source: Greg Smith, age 53.*)

Editor's note: Greg Smith describes this incident in depth during episode 28 of the AAC's Sharp End *podcast.*

NEW HAMPSHIRE

FALL ON ICE | Inadequate Tool Placements
Cannon Cliff, Black Dike

On February 4, a team of climbers from Amherst, Massachusetts, was ascending the third and final pitch of the Black Dike (WI4 M3), Cannon Cliff's most popular ice climb. As the leader (male, age 47) moved up the final ice before the route turns to névé, both of his tools popped and he fell—first onto an ice bulge about 20 feet down and then farther down the ice until an ice screw he had placed held the fall. Rescuers estimate he fell 60 feet in total, breaking a lower leg.

The belayer lowered the injured climber down to his belay stance at the fixed anchor on the top of the second pitch. Climbers who were below on the Black Dike and on the nearby Fafnir rushed to assist the injured leader and dialed 911. New Hampshire Fish and Game, in addition to volunteer rescuers and a pair of guides who had just finished working for the day, hiked up from the parking lot with a sled, bringing the total number of rescuers to 14. The injured climber was attached to a volunteer with a rescue spider and lowered down the second pitch. Rescuers then completed a 120-meter lower down the first pitch and a snow slope at the base. They placed the patient in the litter and lowered and carried him down about

Rescuers working at the base of the Black Dike on Cannon Cliff, still about 1,000 vertical feet above the trail. *Bob Hall*

1,000 vertical feet of snow and talus to the bike path below, about five hours after the fall. A snowmobile then carried him to the road.

ANALYSIS

The Black Dike, a climb that receives no sun, is often prone to brittle, "dinner-plating" ice. Moreover, the heavy traffic this route receives creates a latticework of fractured ice. Extra care must be taken when moving on ice tool and crampon placements.

Using more frequent, gentle swings—instead of a few hard hits—in brittle ice helps to keep tool placements where they belong. Keeping picks, crampons, and ice screws sharp and not climbing above bad placements helps keep winter climbing from spinning out of control. Ice screws work well as protection, but this doesn't stop the relatively low angle of most ice climbs from creating serious falling hazard. (*Source: Michael Wejchert, Mountain Rescue Service.*)

THREE FALLS ON ROCK | Protection Pulled Out
Cathedral Ledge and Kancamagus Highway

On July 10, two climbers headed to the Barber Wall, a single-pitch crack climbing area on the upper left side of Cathedral Ledge. The pair decided to get on Nutcracker, a popular 5.10a. The leader (male, 30s) placed a number 2 Camalot, followed by two small cams below a little overlap or overhang. In order to protect the upper part of the climb, he back-cleaned the number 2. As he attempted the overlap, he fell. Both of the remaining cams ripped out and the climber fell to the ground, 30 feet below, hitting his belayer in the process.

A nearby climber responded to the accident and called for help. Shortly thereafter, the North Conway Fire Department and volunteers from the Mountain Rescue Service arrived and carried the patient in a litter up to the parking lot and tourist overlook on top of Cathedral Ledge, roughly 200 feet above the Barber Wall. The climber sustained minor fractures to vertebrae, a broken rib, and a lung contusion.

On October 2, an aid climber (male, 30s) was leading the first pitch of a potential new route at the Painted Wall, a cliff off the Kancamagus Highway. Though it was not this climber's first time up the pitch, on this occasion a piton ripped out as he weighted it, and the force of his fall pulled out two more pitons and an Alien cam. The climber estimated he fell 15 to 18 feet before landing on the ground, seemingly injuring his leg (subsequent X-rays revealed a hairline fracture on his pelvis).

The pair of climbers telephoned two friends who came to help, and the four of them attempted to hike down the talus field at the base of the Painted Wall to the parking lot. When it became clear that self-evacuation was not an option due to the patient's pain level, the climbers called Mountain Rescue Service, who packaged the victim in a litter and carried him to the road.

On the weekend of October 14, two climbers hiked to Woodchuck Ledge, also on the Kancamagus Highway, to attempt Screaming Yellow Zonkers, a 5.11c crack climb. The leader (male, 20s) fell a couple of times onto small cams at the crux near the top of the pitch. On his next fall, two small cams (number 1 and 2 Metolius Ultralight Master Cams) pulled out of the crack. The next piece down, an 0.3 Camalot, stopped his fall, but he still hit the ground with rope stretch, suffering a fractured wrist and a separated shoulder. New Hampshire Fish and Game responded, as well as another pair of climbers who were on the scene, and the injured climber was carried out of the woods in a litter.

ANALYSIS

Though separate incidents, these three falls have some things in common: Each occurred when relatively small gear placements failed, and each involved experienced climbers. Even for knowledgeable trad climbers, protecting small cracks requires more patience and practice, and sometimes simply requires more gear. Building equalized nests of small pieces and "overprotecting" the start of climbs is often what it takes to keep a leader from hitting the ground.

The Barber Wall has been the scene of four ground falls since 2014. Three of these occurred because of gear placements failing. However, unlike the neighboring climb Double Vee, which has seen two ground falls in as many years, Nutcracker should be straightforward to protect.

It's notable that both the Nutcracker and Screaming Yellow Zonkers leaders broke their helmets in their falls—it's likely the helmets prevented other serious injuries. Because of quick response by nearby climbers and rescue organizations, all three patients reached medical care with relative speed. Cell phones work in select spots off the Kancamagus and at other backcountry New Hampshire crags. However, carrying an inReach or similar satellite communication device and a light first-aid kit is not a bad idea for the more remote cliffs of the Northeast. (*Source: Michael Wejchert, Mountain Rescue Service.*)

NEW YORK

FALL ON ICE | Fatigue, Dehydration
Adirondacks, Chapel Pond

A climber on the crux of Rhiannon, above the sloping ledge where Matt Horner impacted. *Jim Lawyer*

I took a 40-foot fall on ice at Chapel Pond, smashed my face, and suffered a traumatic brain injury, but lived to tell about it. It was February 8, and I was guiding Rhiannon, a 200-foot WI4+ line in the Power Play amphitheater, above Chapel Pond. It was a warm day, and I was not feeling well as we headed up to the base. I was moving so slowly while getting ready that my client asked me if I was okay. I told her I didn't feel great, but I figured I'd be fine as soon as I started climbing.

A lot of people climb Rhiannon in two pitches, but I usually do it in one with 70-meter half ropes. The first part of the climb is a steep slab up to a ledge, then a long vertical piece with a short, steep headwall at the very top.

The ice was wet above the ledge, and I didn't want my client to have to stop in the dripping ice to take out protection, so I placed my last screw at the ledge (that's normally how I climb the route anyway). About 20 feet above the ledge, I stopped just below the steepest part of the climb and got ready to place another screw. My tools were firmly planted when it happened: My brain shut down—I short-circuited and blacked out. I didn't blow out any ice, my tools didn't pop, my feet didn't pop. I literally just let go of my tools for a split second. I came to immediately and was very confused. I knew I was falling, but I didn't know why. I had enough time to think, "This is not going to be good."

My client said that, watching from below, it looked like I was climbing normally and then she saw my body kind of slump, and then I was off.

I fell about 40 feet and smashed into the ice, face-first, and then slid another 10 to 20 feet. I'm sure there was some rope stretch, as there always is with half ropes. You always fall a lot farther than you think you're going to. When I hit the ledge I got knocked out, I don't know for how long, and then I woke up. My first thought when I came to was, "OK, I'm alive." My second thought was "Holy, s***, there's a lot of blood."

My client lowered me to the base and untied me from the rope, and I got up and walked out with her. At the hospital in Burlington, Vermont, the doctors said I had a cerebral hemorrhage and I had broken every plate in my face; I broke my nose in 10 places. I also had some minor soft-tissue injuries. Luckily, my face has healed, and I didn't need reconstructive surgery. My brain continues to heal.

ANALYSIS

I'm still not sure why I blacked out, but it was probably a combination of things. I was pushing really hard last season, climbing in the backcountry a lot and just pushing, pushing, pushing. I may have been quite dehydrated as well, and I wasn't eating well, especially for that kind of output. After my hospitalization, in a follow-up appointment, I had my Vitamin D level tested and it was very low. I don't know if that had anything to do with the accident, but I'm on a supplement now. I've also changed my diet and lost weight. I'm back to climbing hard routes and guiding.

If there's a lesson here, it's take care of yourself and pay attention to how you feel. I always had a tendency to push through things and say, "I'll be fine." And this day I knew I wasn't feeling well. This accident made me think about my health and also got me into a renewed frame of mind. It's sort of like, "Wow, I got another shot, let's try to be a little smarter about this." (*Source: Matt Horner.*)

Editor's note: Working guides often run it out to make seconding easier for their clients, but the consequences of a mistake or outside factors (rockfall, illness, etc.) can be severe, not just for the guide but potentially the client as well.

ADIRONDACKS AND CATSKILLS SUMMARY: *There were four technical climbing rescues in the mountains of upstate New York in 2017. In addition to the one described above, a 58-year-old man fell on an ice climb in Platte Clove in the Catskills and was injured but able to walk out with assistance; two climbers were stranded on Wallface, a remote cliff in the High Peaks, after dropping their rope; and a soloist was stranded about 70 feet up Shipton's Arête (5.4) at Chapel Pond.*

FALL ON ROCK | Inadequate Protection
Shawangunks, The Trapps

On October 14, I started leading the direct start to Ventre de Boeuf, which begins with an easy squeeze chimney leading to a short 5.10 offwidth. Because of the chimney start, my first piece of pro was a number 4 Camalot maybe 20 feet off the deck. I tried working the offwidth move for a bit, but ultimately found it to be a little too slimy and hard. The regular 5.9 start avoids this offwidth by climbing up a thin crack maybe 12 feet to the right. Because I didn't want to yard on the cam to bypass the OW section (as it was my only pro), and not wanting to take a pendulum swing if I fell off the line to the right, I removed the cam, downclimbed a bit, and then started traversing up and to the right to join the regular start.

I found only two marginal pieces of pro: a small offset nut and then a sort of upward-facing number 0.1 (red) Black Diamond X4 cam. These pieces were about 1.5 feet apart from one another. As I was making a move maybe two feet from where I could reach with my left hand to the crack above the offwidth, my foot blew, along with the two small pieces of pro. I instinctively kicked out from the wall when the cam blew, and I think that zippered out my nut.

I fell about 16 to 18 feet and briefly landed upright on my feet, but most of the impact was absorbed on my right butt and right hand. I was wearing a helmet and didn't hit my head. I suffered two compression fractures (L1 and L2) and a good deal of trauma to my lower abs and pelvic area (although thankfully didn't break my pelvis), and I needed a few stitches in my right palm.

The wide crack is the 5.10 direct start to Ventre de Boeuf. The usual 5.9 PG-13 start is just to the right. *Eric Ratkowski*

ANALYSIS

In retrospect, I should have kept the big cam in. I would have pendulumed into the corner if I fell, but this likely would have been much better than hitting the ground. I hate placing nuts as the first pro, but the pickings were slim. (*Source: Daniel Negless.*)

SHAWANGUNKS ANNUAL SUMMARY
Mohonk Preserve

In 2017 there were 16 reported climbing-related accidents at the Mohonk Preserve. These resulted in four head injuries, one spinal fracture, four long-bone fractures, three shoulder dislocations, and minor ankle, wrist, and hand injuries. Ten accidents required technical rescues.

Five of the injuries were sustained due to one or more pieces of protection failing to hold during a lead fall. Three climbers suffered injuries while soloing or prior to placing protection.

One climber was injured twice, in two separate falls, while attempting Westward Ha!, a popular 5.7 in the Millbrook area. The climber was about 40 feet up when a large hold pulled out, striking him in the foot. After his fall, the climber downclimbed to the Grand Traverse Ledge (the start of the climb, accessed by rappel) and assessed the injury with his partner. Concluding the injury was minor, the climber decided to make another attempt. After clearing the first roof in the corner, he fell again—this time an inverted fall of approximately 60 feet, during which the climber made contact with the cliff face, causing serious injury to the right hand.

The climber was stabilized and secured on Grand Traverse Ledge by his partner, who then ascended to the high point and continued to the cliff top on a self-belay. During this process, while attempting to call rangers for assistance, the partner dropped his cell phone, but hikers passing by were able to contact the rangers. Meanwhile, the injured climber began slowly ascending the fixed line. Once on scene, rangers hauled the climber up the remaining distance, treated his injury, and transported the party back to their vehicles.

There was a reported incident of a climber in the Near Trapps who was climbing alone and ran into trouble while self-lowering. [*After finishing a route, instead of rappelling, the climber threaded his rope through a fixed anchor, tied back in, and then used an ATC-style device on the other strand to lower himself from the anchor.*] When still far above the ground, he noticed there was not enough rope to reach the bottom of the climb and immediately stopped; it was reported the climber did not have a stopper knot in the system and had less than a foot of rope remaining below his belay device. A local climber heard a call for help and found the climber hanging in space. The local soloed up above the stuck climber, set up an anchor, rappelled to the climber, and helped him to the ground.

Two climbers at the Trapps were stranded when they failed to untie a stopper knot before attempting to pull their rappel rope down to an intermediate rappel station. The rope end became stuck above. The two climbers had no headlamps or warm clothing, and were unable to ascend the rope to fix the problem. A Mohonk Preserve ranger scrambled to the top of the Trapps, lowered headlamps to the climbers, and removed the stopper knot. The climbers then safely rappelled to the ground.

As mentioned above, several accidents occurred at the Mohonk Preserve when protection failed to hold during a fall. Typically, these accidents occur due to placements being set at an inappropriate angle for the direction of pull during a fall. We must always consider how forces change throughout a pitch and how each piece of gear will respond when loaded.

In 2017, several climbers were able to self-rescue, having the skills and equipment to adjust and adapt when things went wrong. Some were not prepared and required rescue. A skilled climber builds self-rescue into his or her portfolio of technical skills; the ability to escape a loaded belay or ascend a tensioned rope can be invaluable. (*Source: Andrew Bajardi, Chief Ranger, Mohonk Preserve.*)

NORTH CAROLINA

LOWERING ERROR | Rope Pulled Through Device, No Helmet
Hanging Rock State Park, Moore's Wall

Late in the afternoon on April 16, a male climber (28) was injured after falling approximately 20 feet to the ground in the Moore's Wall Amphitheater while being lowered from the route Quaker State (5.11a). The belayer's end of the rope slipped through the belay device before the climber reached the ground, precipitating the fall. The patient was conscious when EMS arrived and complained of head pain. Upon arriving at the hospital, the climber was diagnosed with a fractured temporal bone and cerebral hemorrhage in the back of his head. He was not wearing a helmet. (*Source: Hanging Rock State Park.*)

ANALYSIS

This route is about 100 feet high, so lowering with a 60-meter (197-foot) rope would provide no margin for error. Although the precise circumstances are not known, ropes shrink with age, making it possible the climbers' rope was shorter than believed. It's also possible that the method the climber used to thread the anchors for lowering used up significant amounts of rope.

This type of incident continues to be a problem at climbing areas across the country. These accidents can be prevented by closing the belay system, which can be done by: (1) Both climber and belayer tying into the rope; (2) Placing a stopper knot on the end of the rope; and/or (3) Tying the belayer's end of the rope to an anchor or rope bag. And, always wear a helmet. (*Source: The Editors.*)

RAPPEL ERROR | Uneven Ropes, Inexperience, No Helmet
Pilot Mountain State Park

On October 21, JM (40) attempted a rappel from the top of the climb Honey Pot (5.5), located in the Three Bears area. As she rappelled, one end of the rope passed through her device and she fell approximately 30 feet, hitting a ledge, and then fell to the ground, striking her head. Climbers with medical training were on the scene immediately and were able to perform basic first aid. EMTs arrived on site approximately 30 minutes later. She was conscious immediately after the fall. She had a large head laceration, four missing teeth and two fractured neck vertebrae. She was not wearing a helmet.

Multiple witnesses noted seeing JM at the top of the rock face and saw her throw her rope down to rappel. They also reported noticing that the doubled rope was uneven and that one end did not reach the ground but ex-

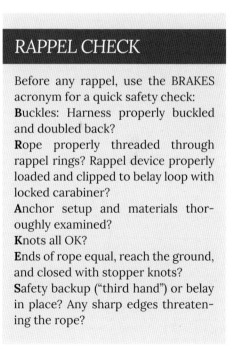

RAPPEL CHECK

Before any rappel, use the BRAKES acronym for a quick safety check:
Buckles: Harness properly buckled and doubled back?
Rope properly threaded through rappel rings? Rappel device properly loaded and clipped to belay loop with locked carabiner?
Anchor setup and materials thoroughly examined?
Knots all OK?
Ends of rope equal, reach the ground, and closed with stopper knots?
Safety backup ("third hand") or belay in place? Any sharp edges threatening the rope?

tended only about 10 feet down from the anchors. All witnesses stated that the time between noticing her rope being uneven and when she began the rappel was only a matter of seconds and that no one could stop her before she came to the short end of the rope and it passed through her device.

The climber failed to ensure both ends of the rope were on the ground before beginning to rappel. She also did not tie stopper knots on the rope ends. She had been told by her partner earlier in the day not to set up an anchor unless someone else was there to observe. Another witness watched her set up a top anchor earlier in the day, and although it was set up correctly, the witness said she displayed a lack of safety awareness as she worked at the top of the rock face.

It's apparent that JM rushed the rappel setup and moved quickly onto the ropes. For critical transitions like going on a rappel, take an extra moment to verify everything is correct. In addition, if JM had yelled "Rope!" or "On rappel!" to the climbers below before starting down, this might have given them additional opportunity to warn her. Experienced climbers need to speak up immediately when they observe a technique or behavior that puts a climber in imminent danger. (*Sources: Karsten Delap, Pilot Mountain State Park, and Aram Attarian.*)

OREGON

FALL ON ICE | Failure to Self-Arrest, Inadequate Equipment
Mount Hood

At 10:40 a.m. on May 7, John Jenkins (32) was ascending the South Side (Hogsback) route on Mt. Hood when he slipped on ice above the bergschrund and was unable to self-arrest. He was unroped at the time and fell approximately 600 feet into the Devil's Kitchen area, sustaining multiple serious injuries.

A number of climbers, including an emergency room physician and an EMT, assisted in his care. A 911 cell phone call activated rescue resources, and a Portland Mountain Rescue team arrived on scene within an hour. An Oregon Army National Guard Blackhawk helicopter performed a hoist evacuation 4.5 hours after the fall, but Jenkins' medical condition deteriorated rapidly, and he succumbed to his injuries prior to reaching Legacy Emanuel Medical Center.

ANALYSIS
The cause of the fall is unknown. The climber's inability to self-arrest the fall may be attributed to inadequate equipment. Jenkins was using ski poles with self-arrest grips at the time of the fall. His ice axe was strapped on his backpack. During icy conditions, a self-arrest ski pole is no substitute for an axe. Roped climbing and anchored belays should also be considered in these conditions. (*Source: Portland Mountain Rescue.*)

GROUND FALL | Quickdraw Unclipped From Bolt
Smith Rock, The Dihedrals

On June 30, a male climber (age 40) was attempting Helium Woman (5.9) when he fell and impacted the ground, fracturing both of his ankles. He had stick-clipped the second bolt and had climbed up and right to a point between the second and the third bolt when he asked his belayer (age unknown) to "take." He waited for slack to be removed, then let go of the rock with the expectation of a short lead fall, but instead fell to the ground. The quickdraw had come unclipped from the second bolt during the fall and was found by the climber underneath him after he landed. It is believed it was still attached to the rope. (*Source: Deschutes County Sheriff's Office Search and Rescue.*)

ANALYSIS

It seems likely that one of two possibilities occurred. First, the upper carabiner of the quickdraw might have been insufficiently clipped (nose clipped) to the second bolt. This can occur when tape or a stick is used to keep the carabiner gate open for stick-clipping. After stick-clipping a bolt, always visually confirm that the carabiner is properly attached to the bolt hanger and the gate is completely shut.

    The other possibility (considered most likely) is the rope rotated the upper carabiner in such a way that it levered against the bolt hanger and unclipped as the climber moved to the right and/ or the belayer took in slack. Assembling quick-draws with both carabiner gates oriented in the same direction and clipping draws so the gates are oriented away from the direction of travel will minimize the chances of a carabiner gate le-vering open against a bolt hanger. When there is only one bolt between you and a long ground fall on a sport climb (as when stick-clipping the second bolt), consider using a quickdraw with two locking carabiners for that crucial clip. (*Source: Deschutes County SAR and the Editors.*)

In rare cases, it's possible for a carabiner gate to lever against a bolt and unclip. The top biner in this draw should be oriented in the same direction as the rope biner. *Erik Rieger*

STRANDED IN MIDAIR | Inadequate Protection
Smith Rock, Northwest Face

On September 30, three climbers (one male, two female, ages 27 to 31) were climb-ing Wherever I May Roam, a popular five-pitch sport route (5.9) on the northwest face. One of them led the third pitch, traversing up and left to an anchor on an arête. When the next climber followed, she removed all the quickdraws on the pitch. The third climber then started the pitch. She fell, and due to the travers-ing nature of the pitch and lack of protection, pendulumed left and away from the route and into midair. The leader was belaying both climbers directly off the anchor using a device in plaquette mode ("guide mode") and was unable to raise or lower the climber after her fall. She remained suspended until another party on the route arrived to assist. (*Source: Deschutes County Sheriff's Office Search and Rescue.*)

ANALYSIS

In a party of three, it's partly the second climber's job to ensure the third climber is adequately protected against swinging falls on traverses and roofs. This pendulum fall could have been avoided by the second climber leaving all the quickdraws in place and making sure the third climber's rope was clipped to each of them.

Leaders transitioning to multi-pitch routes need to be familiar with a number of skills not needed in single-pitch climbing, including self-rescue. The use of a belay device in plaquette mode should be accompanied by the knowledge required to safely perform a weighted release and lower. If this could have been accomplished, the party could have lowered the third climber to bolted anchors directly below the third-pitch anchor on this climb. They then could have rappelled with her to the ground. If the climber had the appropriate gear and skills, she also could have ascended the rope to the upper belay. (*Source: Deschutes County SAR and the Editors.*)

FALL ON ROCK | Inattentive Belay
Smith Rock, Smith Rock Group, Northeast Face

On November 21 at around 11 a.m., two experienced climbers were attempting a multi-pitch sport route called Lost in Space (5.10b). Climber 1 (male, age 28) was leading the third pitch of the route. After clipping the third bolt, a foothold broke, causing him to fall approximately 15 feet, hit the belay ledge, knock off a large chunk of rock, and continue to fall an additional five feet before being caught by his belayer. The climber sustained injuries to his left ankle that were later diagnosed as a non-displaced fracture of the talus and calcaneus. Climber 2, the belayer (male, age 35), was clear of the path of the falling rock and escaped unharmed.

The climbers were using a 60-meter rope, which was of insufficient length for rappelling to the ground from their location. Climber 2 led the rest of the climb and assisted his injured partner up the remaining pitches to the top, from which they descended by an established rappel route.

ANALYSIS

Despite being friends for a number of years, the two had only climbed together on rare occasions. Prior to the day of the accident, they had climbed for two days at Smith Rock. During this time, Climber 1 reported noticing Climber 2 had a nonchalant attitude toward belaying (e.g. sitting down, excessive slack in the system) but did not express his discomfort with these belay methods. While on Lost in Space, Climber 2 sat on the belay ledge with his back to the Climber 1 and doled out slack at regular intervals without being cognizant of the amount of slack in the system and the climber's position on the wall. Climber 1 had just clipped the third bolt, above his waist, when the foothold broke and initiated the fall. With appropriate slack in the system, he should have fallen only about five feet.

The takeaway here is to speak up if a climber is concerned about the belayer's technique, including maintaining positive control of the brake strand of the rope, maintaining visual contact with the climber on the wall, and adjusting the slack in the system to avoid ledge falls. (*Source: Climber 1.*)

ESSENTIALS

EVACUATE AN INJURED PARTNER
THE SPLIT-COIL ROPE LITTER

By R. Bryan Simon

One of the most common injuries for climbers during a fall is a sprain or break of the lower leg. An easy morning hike to the crag can turn into an evening epic if a partner has injured a leg. The following techniques may allow a small team to evacuate an injured partner without additional help.

As with all accidents, assess the fallen climber for life-threatening injuries and address any of these first (think ABCs—airway, breathing, circulation—as well as head trauma and massive bleeding) before evacuating. If the climber has no life-threatening injuries and you are not concerned about any head or spine injury, the one-person or two-person rope litter can greatly increase your ability to evacuate an injured partner.

Both of these litters are easy to construct and allow the injured climber to be carried in a "piggyback" fashion. The rope distributes the climber's weight to the rescuer's shoulders and hips, much like a backpack.

Rope carries can be used in any terrain, though care should be taken in talus, and other techniques might be better in loose scree. By distributing the weight effectively, these techniques also allow lighter climbers to carry significantly heavier partners for some distance.

ONE-PERSON SPLIT-COIL ROPE LITTER

The first step to create this litter is to coil your rope into a single-strand butterfly (backpack) coil, beginning with the rope running over your shoulders and one end of the rope touching the ground. Continue coiling your rope until there is roughly two meters remaining. Ideally you want all of the coils to be equal in length, settling to just above your hips, as these loops will distribute your partner's weight across each strand.

Next, carefully lay the coil on your rope mat or the ground. Take the initial length (the end that touched the ground) and bring it to the center to create another coil loop. Using the other end of the rope (two-

Insert rescuer's arms through each end of the coils to make a seat for an injured climber. *R. Bryan Simon*

meter portion), create a final coil and use the remainder of the length to create a tight finishing wrap several times around the center of the coils, tucking the tail back through these wraps and tightening to secure the litter. This final wrap will become the injured climber's seat.

Pad the coils around the shoulders with whatever is available for comfort, and use a sling and a carabiner to secure the two coils at your chest, like a chest strap on a backpack.

To get your partner into the litter, it is easiest to get them to lean against the wall or a nearby tree. Put one coil over your shoulder and snake the remainder behind your partner and then place the other coil over your opposite shoulder. Make sure the wrapped section is located beneath your partner's buttocks. Carefully stand up. The patient's legs should go to each side of the rescuer, with his or her inner thighs directly against the rescuer's flanks, as if being carried "piggyback." Attach the sling and carabiner.

TWO-PERSON SPLIT-COIL ROPE LITTER

This litter is similar to that above, but can be used by two people. While distributing the injured climber's weight between two people is a huge advantage, this technique can be difficult to maneuver "three wide" on narrow trails. It is also difficult if the height of the two rescuers is greatly different; when heights are different, situate the coil "seat" to the side of the shorter climber to allow for better weight distribution.

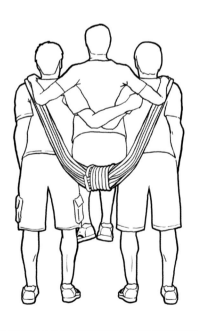

The two-person rope litter. *Vertical Medicine Resources*

To create an effective two-person carry, coil the rope into slightly longer coils so that it allows the injured climber to sit between the rescuers at the level of their hips. Each rescuer should place a coil over their head and on top of their outside shoulder. Again, pad the coils for comfort.

A few final points. Dynamic ropes will stretch somewhat with the weight of the climber, and litters may need to be recoiled during longer evacuations. In cold conditions the injured climber needs to be well insulated, as he or she will not be active during the evacuation.

"Ropes to the Rescue: Climber Evacuation Techniques," by R. Bryan Simon, in *Wilderness Medicine*, March 2015 (available online), includes step-by-step photos of this technique.

FALL ON DESCENT | Loose Rock
North Sister

On August 12, a male climber (age 49) fell while descending the North Sister via the South Ridge (Grade II, Class 4) after summiting the peak with a group of 11 climbers from a local climbing club. The accident occurred in the "Bowling Alley," a loose, steep gully, when he stepped onto a boulder that shifted. This caused him to fall onto his back just downhill of the boulder, which then rolled over his outstretched right arm. He sustained a fractured ulna and displaced ulna and radius (lower arm bones) at the elbow. Other members of the group splinted the injured extremity and called 911. Deschutes County Search and Rescue responded and assisted the group's descent to the southeast ridge, from which a helicopter flew the injured climber to a local medical center.

ANALYSIS

In areas of loose scree and boulders, climbers must remain attentive throughout the descent, but some accidents of this type are practically unavoidable. This party was organized by a local climbing club and was well-led and prepared, including some members with medical training. They were able to treat and begin evacuating the injured climber and likely would have been able to self-rescue had outside assistance not been available. (*Source: Deschutes County Sheriff's Office Search and Rescue.*)

STRANDED | Suspected Hypothermia
Cascades, Three Fingered Jack

On the afternoon of August 13, a female climber (21) and her brother (25) became disoriented while descending Three Fingered Jack when heavy fog blanketed the area. [The standard south ridge route on Three Fingered Jack (7,844') has a couple of hundred feet of scrambling and low fifth-class rock just below the top.] Due to near zero visibility, the pair got off route and reached a point where they were unable to ascend or descend safely. They called for help in late afternoon. A rescue team located the siblings at 1:25 a.m., and, after assessing their medical status, airlifted the female climber due to a possible shoulder injury. Team members descended with the male climber. (*Source: Corvallis Mountain Rescue Unit.*)

ANALYSIS

Conditions in the mountains change rapidly, and climbers should prepare by researching a route thoroughly and carrying adequate clothing, equipment, food, and water for an unexpected night out. (*Source: Corvallis Mountain Rescue Unit and The Editors.*)

THE 10 ESSENTIALS

Navigation (map, altimeter, compass, GPS device with batteries)
Headlamp (extra batteries)
Sun protection
First-aid kit
Knife
Fire (matches, lighter with tinder, stove)
Shelter (bivy sack, tent)
Extra food
Extra water (or purification)
Extra clothes
Source: *Freedom of the Hills*, 2017 Edition

UTAH

FATAL FALL FROM ANCHOR | Miscommunication
Wasatch Range, Big Cottonwood Canyon

On July 13, Matt Hearn (26) was climbing High Fructose Corn Syrup, a long single-pitch 5.8 at the Slips, a popular Salt Lake beginner area. When Hearn reached the top of the route, his belayer and a few others on the ground thought they heard him call "off belay." His belayer took him off, and shortly afterward Hearn fell approximately 115 feet to the ground, hitting his head on rocks at the base. Nearby climbers performed CPR, but Hearn died on the scene.

ANALYSIS

It would be somewhat surprising for the climber to go off belay at the top of this route because the anchor is equipped with fixed steel carabiners, so lowering is the norm and there is no need to untie and thread the anchor. It seems likely this was a case of miscommunication. This crag has many routes closely spaced to one another, and it's possible the belayer and others on the ground heard a nearby climber give an off-belay command. It's also possible Hearn miscommunicated his intent before climbing.

Always tell your belayer how you plan to descend a route before starting up it. Minimize extraneous conversation or commands at an anchor, and only say "off belay" if you are going off to rappel or belay your partner from above. When climbing in busy areas, be sure to use names with your commands—"Off belay, Jen!" rather than just "off belay"—so your partner knows that you specifically made a given command. (*Source: The Editors.*)

FALL ON ROCK | Loose Rock, Inadequate Protection
Wasatch Range, Big Willow Cirque

On June 10, my partner Chloe (22) and I (23), both experienced climbers, hiked three to four hours to Big Willow Cirque, high above Salt Lake City. After three trips into this beautiful area that season, I had spotted a new line on a cliff we dubbed the Forbidden Wall.

After a steep snow approach to the base, we begin climbing in beautiful weather around 11 a.m. The first pitch had fun and engaging climbing on decent granite for about 180 feet. Pitch two looked moderate but had few options for protection. Having climbed many pitches like this, I confidently set off. Twenty feet above the belay ledge, I placed a cam and continued. Another 15 feet led to a tipped-out cam placement behind a loose flake, then another 10 feet to a stance where I tried to put in another piece. As I was placing the gear, the rock under my foot broke and I fell. The cam below me blew out. Two small ledges slowed the speed of my long fall, which landed me next to my partner, tangled in rope and upside down.

After going in and out of consciousness for the next five minutes, I came to. Chloe was able to assist in untangling me from the rope. She assessed me for injuries and head trauma. My helmet was intact but dented from the fall. A concussion was evident, as I underwent personality changes and severe mood swings after the fall.

We managed to self-rescue off the wall and down the snowfield to our packs. Chloe was able to call friends who knew the area well. A helicopter was called but unable to land, so SAR planned to meet us on the trail. My partner and I started the slow walk out and were met by a trail runner who assisted us for four or five hours until friends met us, followed by SAR lower on the trail.

ANALYSIS

Any decisions in the alpine should be thought out thoroughly, and first ascents in remote territory add layers of risk and complexity, including loose rock, vegetation, and the unknowns of route-finding and protection. Even without passing up any opportunities for protection, there was much less gear than I was comfortable with. We studied a possible variation that was less direct, but it did not look like it would offer any more protection than the line we chose. I should have looked harder for alternatives or perhaps retreated.

I am thankful my partner was a nurse; otherwise, my outcome could have been very different. This fall was also a perfect example of how wearing a helmet can save a life. I feel fortunate only to have sustained a severe concussion and lacerations. (*Source: Madison Goodman.*)

GROUND FALL FROM ANCHORS | Miscommunication
Little Cottonwood Canyon, Coffin Buttress

On March 11 a 27-year-old man led C.P.O.D., a 5.11- crack climb. None of his companions wanted to follow the climb, and since it traverses to the right, the climber decided it would be easiest to descend and then reclimb the pitch on top-rope to clean it. However, the diagonal climb would have made rappelling difficult, and he was reluctant to simply lower because he worried the rough rock would abrade his rope.

Instead, he asked one of his friends to tie into the belayer's end of the rope (the strand running through the protection on the route) to weight it. Using this counter-balance, the climber planned to rappel the other strand of rope to the ground. However, the climber on the ground was relatively inexperienced and did not clearly understand the technique he'd been asked to perform. Instead of tying into and weighting the lead rope, he weighted the strand hanging free from the anchor. The climber above had already installed his rappel device on this strand and did not notice the mistake that had been made below. When he unclipped from the anchor and leaned back, he fell about 50 feet to the ground, pulling the other end of the rope through the gear and the anchor.

Salt Lake County SAR responded and lowered the climber down 800 feet of rough terrain in a litter. The climber had five spinal fractures but no neurological damage.

ANALYSIS

When climbing with beginners or unfamiliar partners, it's best to avoid unorthodox techniques such as this. When unusual steps become necessary, they need to be explained clearly and then double-checked (visually, if possible) by an experienced climber before they are trusted. (*Sources: Online report by the climber and the Editors.*)

MORE LITTLE COTTONWOOD INCIDENTS: *Little Cottonwood experienced a wide range of accidents, including an apparently intoxicated climber who fell 25 to 30 feet to the ground from a sport climb when his belayer failed to catch him. The climber was not wearing a helmet and suffered significant head and shoulder wounds. Various witnesses reported the two had been drinking alcohol for much of the day.*

Two climbers had ankle fractures after falls at Gate Buttress: one while leading the third pitch of a climb and the other (a beginner) while scrambling the 3rd-class approach. One party was stranded on the south ridge of Mt. Superior, a popular long climb (5.4) that is often scrambled; a second had to be rescued from Superior when a September snowstorm caught them. In a bizarre and frightening incident, several climbers in the Pentapitch area reported more than a dozen gunshots aimed at or near them by an unidentified shooter on the road below. No one was hit.

TUMBLING BOULDER ROLLS OVER BELAYER
Moab Area, Day Canyon

On October 11, four climbers and I were cragging in Day Canyon. After warming up on a nearby climb, my partner and I threw our rope down in front of Boognish Tower, a 100-foot chimney climb (5.10-). I tied in on the follower's end and started to belay my partner. I was standing next to a washing machine–size boulder that was slightly up a slope and a few feet to the right of me. I was belaying with a Grigri.

The boulder at right tumbled over the belayer at the base of Boognish Tower.

My partner was about one-third of the way up the route, halfway between two bolts, when I heard "ROCK! ROCK!!!" yelled from behind me. Startled and confused, I saw from the corner of my eye that the large boulder had started to shift down the sandy slope toward me. I moved backward, trying to avoid the boulder, but could not get away in time. The rock hit my right arm, knocked me backward onto the ground, and then rolled over my right leg. The lead rope snagged on the boulder and I was pulled down the hill for about eight feet before the rock rolled free and continued downhill.

The rope on my end was nearly severed. Another climber put the leader on belay so he could continue up to the next bolt and bail. Despite holding my weight as I tumbled, the leader had not gotten pulled off the route and did not get hurt.

I ended up with a dislocated and broken scaphoid (wrist bone) and lacerations on my forearm and between my thumb and pointer finger (where the rope had been). A divot in the boulder or the unevenness or sandiness of the ground where I landed must have saved me from a broken leg as the boulder rolled over me.

ANALYSIS
Most rockfall accidents involve rocks falling from above, and the best protection usually is to move toward the wall for shelter. In this case, I probably should have done the

same, but due to the proximity of the boulder and momentary confusion when I heard "rock!", I made a bad call and moved the wrong way to get out of the boulder's path.

The boulder had appeared to be sturdy, but warning signs were present. There was heavy rain three days before the accident (probably the main reason the boulder dislodged), and a climber's dog had just dug a shallow hole for himself around the base of the boulder. The boulder sat on a sloped, sandy ledge. No matter how solid they look and how unlikely it seems, it's important to be aware that boulders on the ground can suddenly dislodge. (*Source: Anonymous report from the belayer.*)

RAPPEL ANCHOR FAILURE | Trusting Old Gear
Zion National Park, Cerberus Wall

It was May 22, my fourth day living on the outskirts of Zion National Park. I had moved there for a summer job and was taking every opportunity to climb. That evening, my climbing partner and I took the park shuttle to Cerberus Wall. My partner jumped on the local classic Cherry Crack (5.10c), led it comfortably, and I followed to clean it.

I decided it was time to try another classic, Fails of Power (5.10+). I have been trad climbing for at least four years now, and prior to coming to Zion I could climb 5.10 without too much of an issue. I got pretty worked on this route, though. Toward the top, I was pumped and decided to run it out, hoping to get to a good rest and place a piece. It was getting dark (approximately 9:15 p.m.), so I wanted to hurry. My foot slipped, right at the end of the crux, and I took a good 25-foot whipper, ending up facing away from the rock and flipping over at the last minute.

This vintage cam, found in a Zion crack, failed as a makeshift rappel anchor despite testing. *Benton Mitchell*

After the fall, I was feeling really tired and I didn't think I could finish the route that day. I didn't have enough gear to aid to the anchors, either. Right at the base of the crux was a fixed cam, so I went back up the route to my last piece, just above the fixed cam. I clipped my belay loop to the fixed piece and bounce-tested it repeatedly while still clipped into the backup piece above it. I double-checked that the cam was truly fixed in the crack, and everything looked good.

Still clipped to my backup cam, I ran the rope through the old fixed cam, tested it once more, and then removed the backup and shifted all my weight to begin the rappel. About a foot into the rappel the cam popped out. The next thing I knew I was lying on the ground on top of the coiled rope, with rope burns all over. My partner had rope burns on his hands as well. He had been giving me a fireman's belay and tried to catch the rope as I fell.

My hip took most of the blow from the fall, along with my elbow and my heels. Miraculously I was okay, aside from severe bruising, whiplash, and rope burn. My partner ran down to ask the last park shuttle to wait for me. My head was spinning as I packed up my gear, but I did not seem to have a head injury, which was very fortunate. I did not have a helmet and somehow landed in the only flat spot—sharp rocks surrounded the area. We determined the fall was roughly 40 feet.

ANALYSIS

I trusted a single piece of fixed gear in desert sandstone. I didn't know how long it had been there, who had already worked on getting it out, or how strong it was. I believe that when my weight shifted from a somewhat outward pull to a straight downward pull the cam slipped. I understand that the sport we play is a risky one, but was it worth trying to save a little bit of money by not leaving a backup cam? Gear can be replaced, but life cannot. My partner also realized that he should have spoken up and asked me to leave my own gear.

I now have a whole new appreciation for making sure that gear is solid. And for wearing a helmet! (*Source: Benton Mitchell.*)

VERMONT

GROUND FALL FROM ANCHOR | Miscommunication
Lower West Bolton

At approximately 6 p.m. on September 16, I responded to the report of a fatal rock climbing accident at the Lower West Bolton climbing area. I was directed to an ambulance where the two subjects who had been climbing with the deceased (20-year-old Rebecca Ryan, "RR") were waiting. I briefly interviewed LK (19) to get her version of the events before I went to the scene of the accident. The other partner (IH, 21) was present but said very little.

LK indicated that RR was top-roping a route (later determined to be Harvest Moon, 5.7+) while belayed from the bottom of the climb. The climb is approximately 80 feet high, and the top is not visible from the bottom. LK said that RR completed the climb and gave the command "off belay" to indicate that she had secured her-self to the anchor at the top. LK was under the impression that RR was going to rappel down the route, and she removed her harness to await RR's descent. LK then heard RR yell down, "Are you ready?" She then realized that RR may have been expecting her to lower her down the route, and she yelled up that she was not ready and scrambled to put her harness back on. (IH later remembered the events in a very similar way.) Before she could don her harness, LK observed RR free-fall down the cliff, landing at the bottom.

I asked if they had discussed before the climb what method RR was going to use to descend, but she was not clear on that point. I then examined the scene and found the following:

- RR was tied into one end of the rope in a configuration (Figure 8 follow-through knot properly tied through her harness) that would be consistent with climbing the route and being lowered back down to the bottom by her partner. If she was planning on rappelling, the rope would not have been tied in to her harness.

- RR did not have a rappel device on her harness, which would indicate that she did not have an easy way of rappelling down the route. Her options would have been to be lowered by LK or walk off the route around the top of the cliff.
- RR was not wearing a helmet. It was lying on the ground near her pack at the base of the climb.
- At the top of the climb the rope was threaded through the two bolted anchors, consistent with RR's expectation that she would be lowered from the top.

Five days after the accident, a state police detective and I met with LK and IH to review the sequence of events that led up to the accident. We learned that RR was the most experienced of the climbers, and LK and IH had looked to her as the "leader" of the group, though her outdoor experience was limited. LK said she had just bought her first rope, and this was her first outing using it.

The pattern of climbing throughout the day, prior to the accident, had been for the belayer to lower the climber. At no point during the day had anybody rappelled. Nevertheless, both LK and IH remember RR indicating that her intent was to rappel down their final route (where the accident occurred) after cleaning the anchor. (Source: Neil Van Dyke, Department of Public Safety.)

ANALYSIS

This incident strongly reinforces the importance of a climber and belayer clearly communicating a plan for descending from each anchor, especially when the anchor is out of sight (and possibly out of clear hearing range) from the ground.

In some cases, a climber may need to change the descent plan en route. In this case, RR had stated that she planned to rappel but had no device on her harness or the rope when she fell, suggesting she may have forgotten to carry it and thus was forced to change plans once she reached the anchor. Whenever there is such a change of plans, the climber should communicate the new plan as clearly and loudly as possible and wait for acknowledgment from the belayer. Then, the climber should test the lowering system before unclipping from the anchor, making sure the belayer is holding his or her weight. (Source: The Editors.)

WASHINGTON

RAPPEL ERROR | No Backup
North Cascades National Park, Torment-Forbidden Traverse

On the morning of July 21, Susan Bennett, 61, and three partners set out to climb the Torment-Forbidden traverse. They completed the south ridge of Torment, and after a bivy on the ridge between Torment and Forbidden they got a late start the next morning due to overnight rain soaking their gear. They were moving toward Forbidden before noon.

At the notch below the west ridge of Forbidden, the climbers left some of their gear, planning to return this way from the summit before descending into Boston Basin. The climbers broke into two teams, and Bennett's team reached the false

Forbidden Peak from the northwest. The X marks approximate location of rappel accident. *Ron Clausen | Wikipedia*

summit just as the other team was descending from the true summit. After Bennett and her partner hit the summit, they downclimbed the west ridge until the top of a 5.6 pitch. Because they were wearing mountaineering boots, they decided to rappel this section instead of downclimb. They set up a rappel from an existing anchor, using their doubled 8mm to 8.2mm rope. After throwing down the ends, Bennett's partner noted that they had not tied stopper knots and wondered aloud if they should fix this error, but Bennett expressed fear that knots might get caught in the rocks. She had an autoblock cord clipped to her harness, but apparently did not use it for this rappel.

At approximately 4:30 p.m., Bennett started to rappel at a 45° angle from the anchor, apparently attempting to stay on the ridgeline. At a stance about 25 meters down, she lost her footing and began to pendulum. Her partner could not see what happened, but later said he thought Bennett had impacted with the rock slab and was knocked unconscious. After she re-entered his view, the partner saw Bennett start to slide slowly down the rope, and he yelled for her to grab her brake line. She didn't respond and slid off the end of the rope. She struck a ledge and then began a long tumble over the north face of the mountain. Her helmet broke into several pieces and she disappeared into the clouds near the glacier.

In poor visibility, the other two climbers heard Bennett's partner yelling that she'd fallen. They said they would come up to assist him after calling for help. At the notch, they located an inReach device in Bennett's pack and activated it. Once they were all together, the group debated trying to descend to the north to look for Bennett, but felt they did not have the equipment nor time to make an effective search (it was now 5:30 p.m.), and they knew a search and rescue effort already had been initiated. Instead, they descended together toward Boston Basin, carrying Bennett's gear, until they met a National Park Service helicopter. Bennett's body was spotted about 30 feet down in a crevasse on the Forbidden Glacier around 7,100 feet. (*Source: North Cascades National Park incident reports.*)

ANALYSIS

Bennett was an experienced climber and past instructor with the Mountaineers. It is not clear why she skipped safety precautions (third-hand backup, stopper knots) that she usually used, including during a previous rappel on this same trip. To address concerns about stopper knots getting stuck, they could have carried the rappel rope in coils with them (using "saddlebags" or a similar technique) as they descended and then untied the stopper knots once they were off rappel. Although the official reports do not suggest this, it's possible that Bennett was feeling rushed by their late start, the deteriorating weather, and the fact that their climbing companions were moving faster, and thus took unusual shortcuts with the rappel. (*Source: The Editors.*)

MT. BAKER FATALITY: *A 37-year-old man died after falling several hundred feet and landing in a crevasse on the northeast side of Mt. Baker in the afternoon of August 19. The man's partner also fell and was seriously injured; he was rescued by helicopter. The two were at approximately 6,000 feet on the Sholes Glacier when they fell.*

ICE COLLAPSE

North Cascades National Park, Ptarmigan Traverse

On July 30, my climbing partner, Stefan Goldberg (62) and I (67, both highly experienced mountaineers) began the Ptarmigan Traverse, climbing north to south. Our plan was to spend 12 days on the route, go as far as time permitted, and double back to the trailhead after climbing satellite peaks along the route. However, wildfire smoke conspired against us, making navigation and climbing more hazardous, so after five days we decided to retreat toward Kool Aid Lake.

On August 3, we traversed a rock feature called the Red Ledges. When we had crossed this on the way in, a snow ramp had contacted the rock directly and the transition was straightforward. We now found a far different scenario, with a melted-out ramp that created a gap of about eight to ten feet and necessitated a rappel of 15 to 20 feet. Temperatures in nearby Marblemount had exceeded 100°F the last several days, which greatly contributed to the rapid melt-out. A moat barrier now presented itself, and what had once been a snow ramp was now an icy serac or fin with an adjoining snow cornice.

The icy fin in center collapsed and knocked the photographer into a moat just as he rappelled from the Red Ledges above. Fortunately, he had only minor injuries. *Stefan Goldberg*

Thankfully, a climbing party of four who had started the traverse a day ahead of us had left a sling with two carabiners over a rock horn for a rappel. Stefan went first, rappelling about 20 feet into the moat. He placed an ice screw into hard, nearly vertical snow and attached a sling and extra carabiner to this to assist my transition from rock to snow. He then surmounted the snow wall with two front-point kicks, using one ice axe, and started to traverse out of the moat. He was about eight feet left of the ice serac, moving away from it, when, to my horror, I observed a crack open up at the juncture of the serac and snow wall and run directly toward Stefan. As the crack reached him, another crack opened up, perpendicular to the first. Stefan fell straight down into the moat among tumbling snow and ice blocks. It was like watching a horror video in slow motion.

The ice serac tumbled over sideways until it was stopped by contact with the adjacent rock and vertical snow ledge. I feared the serac would break apart and bury Stefan deep in the moat or make contact with the rope, rip out the anchor sling, and pull me down. I could see some daylight in the depths of the moat, and after several seconds of silence Stefan yelled out, "I'm OK." Miraculously, he had suffered only superficial wounds to his arm and minor head and neck discomfort. He climbed the sloping moat with his 60-pound pack, advancing his prusik up the rappel rope as self-protection, then transitioned onto the edge of the newly inverted serac. He placed an ice screw and transitioned back onto solid snow, where he placed a snow picket. I then rappelled to the serac edge, surmounted it, and removed the screw and picket. We traversed the snowfield to an adjacent talus field, where we thanked our creator that we were still alive.

ANALYSIS

The extreme heat undoubtedly played a major role in the instability of the icy serac and snow ramp. Visual inspection revealed no obvious problems, except for the snowy cornice, which Stefan climbed past with no problems. There might have been a better way to get through the moat, but the serac could have fallen whichever way we went. Simply put, we were in the wrong place at the wrong time. On the positive side, we made several good decisions by relying on a good, strong anchor, using a backup prusik on the rappel, and wearing helmets. (*Source: Ed McCord.*)

GLISSADING DEATH BELOW AASGARD PASS: *A 19-year-old man glissaded into a hole in the snowfield below Aasgard Pass on June 4. This hole, which opens in the spring but is hidden from above, has been the scene of several glissading fatalities. Episode 25 of the Sharp End podcast features an interview with another climber who fell into the same hole but survived.*

SIMUL-RAPPELLING ERROR | No Backups
Methow Valley, Goat Wall

About 9:15 a.m. on May 29, Shelby Withington, 20, and three other climbers finished the seventh pitch on Sisyphus, a multi-pitch 5.11 sport route. The group decided to descend there rather than finish the easier last three pitches.

In order to save time, Withington and his crew opted to simul-rappel in pairs rather than do individual rappels. Withington and his partner went first. The two were not in sync, and Withington's partner reached the belay ledge at the top of the sixth pitch first and then apparently let go of his strand of the rope (as one would typically do upon reaching a ledge in a normal, solo rappel). The climbers had not tied stopper knots in the ends of the rope, so the rope slipped through the partner's device, allowing Withington to fall. One of the climbers at the upper anchor attempted to grab the rope as it pulled through the anchor and was seriously burned but unable to stop the rope. Withington fell about 300 feet before he struck a ledge, then fell another 200 feet or so to the base of the climb. Another team preparing to climb Sisyphus witnessed the accident and called 911. A rescue team helped Withington's partners descend. (*Sources: Okanogan Search and Rescue and published accounts.*)

Simul-rappelling relies on counterbalance, with each side of the rope weighted simultaneously and continuously. Withington and his partner could have ensured they were descending at the same speed and arrived at the ledge at the same time, so they could unweight the system together. A stopper knot and/or friction-hitch backup on the partner's rope might have prevented the rope from slipping through his device.

Simul-rappelling has been the cause of several fatalities in recent years. Although it is theoretically faster than rappelling one at a time, the extra care that must be taken to ensure a safe simul-rappel erases much of that benefit. It is not a recommended technique. (*Source: The Editors.*)

ROCKFALL
Methow Valley, Goat Wall

On June 2, Jason (45) and I (37) set out to climb the 11 pitches of Prime Rib of Goat (5.9). The sun was out, wind was mild, and we both felt confident in our ability. Starting the fourth pitch (the first 5.9 pitch), I was belaying while Jason led. I had used a clove hitch in the climbing rope to tie into a locking carabiner on the anchor. I was positioned close to my anchor in a comfortable spot.

Jason clipped three or four bolts and began to move over the first crux, a small roof. He tested some rock above, but when he went to weight it a large slab (maybe 500 pounds) sheered off directly over my head. He yelled "rock!" several times, and I looked up, grabbed the anchor rope, and jumped closer into the wall where I could protect half to two-thirds of my body. The slab hit the shelf above, hit my helmet with a glancing blow, glanced off my back, and came to rest against my right leg. A basketball-size rock then came down and pinned my right leg into the larger slab.

I lowered Jason, and he tied back into the anchor, checked our gear for damage, and then he did a full check on me. My right leg was bleeding, and my back was in pain, but I could move. We got settled a bit, then rappelled off the route. I ended up with some small chunks missing from my helmet, a badly bruised and scraped-up right leg, and a broken rib in my back, directly below my right scapula.

ANALYSIS

I likely would not have even been touched by the falling rocks if I had been able to get one foot farther away. Having thought through a potential escape while I was belaying might have allowed that. We should have been more aware that rockfall can be more prevalent in springtime. We were coming out of a freeze/thaw cycle, and the chance of larger chunks of rock giving way is more significant. (*Source: Tim, the belayer.*)

FALL ON SNOW | Inexperience, Poor Snow Conditions
Mt. Rainier National Park, Little Tahoma, Fryingpan Glacier

On July 8, we started hiking along Fryingpan Creek and made it to camp above Meany Crest, at around 7,500 feet, by midafternoon. The next day, we woke up at

1 a.m. and started our ascent of Little Tahoma (11,138 feet). We reached the summit around 8:30 a.m. and returned to camp around 3:30 p.m., then took an hour to pack up for the hike out.

We planned to use crampons and ice axes for the descent of the snowfield below camp. I insisted on hauling the glacier rope down, pushing my pack weight to more than 50 pounds. The snow was slushy. We went at our own pace, with the more experienced members of our team in the front. I brought up the rear, and by the time we reached the slope's crest, the climbing party was committed to the slope. Three team members who had nearly reached the bottom saw a crevasse running along the full width of our slope and flagged everyone to traverse back east toward the rocks.

Path of climber's slide toward crevasse, impact site (X) on far side, and continued slide. *Don Sarver Collection*

I was about to yell to our climb leader that I didn't feel safe when my footing gave way. My ice axe was plunged into the snow nearly to its head as a self-belay, but the snow was so slushy that it ripped out of the slope. I tried to self-arrest, and my speed slowed somewhat, but then the sliding snow pushed me down. During the slide, my axe was ripped out of my hands twice but the leash kept it attached. The slope flattened out and I hit a 10- to 12-foot gap, catapulted over it, landed on my back, and kept sliding. About 100 feet past the crevasse, I came to a complete stop.

I performed an assessment of potential injuries and found a serious laceration on my left forearm. I used my ice axe leash to improvise a tourniquet above the injury. My right leg below the knee felt painful, and I couldn't put any pressure on the leg. I never lost consciousness.

A member of our team activated a personal locator beacon (PLB), and another called 911. The team shoveled out a flat platform in the snow, stabilized my injuries, and kept me warm in my sleeping bag. About 90 minutes after the accident, I was airlifted off the mountain. My injuries included a severely sprained right ankle, compression fractures in my L4 and L5 lumbar vertebrae, and a deep laceration on my left forearm.

ANALYSIS

Several things contributed to the accident. I was inexperienced in descending steep, snow-covered slopes. We didn't scout the descent route in advance, and by the time we all saw the crevasse and how serious it was, we were already on the slope. It's possible that if we had known about the existence of the crevasse, we might have chosen a different descent route.

We descended late in the day when the snow was slushy. This made for very unstable footing and insecure axe placements. I also used incorrect self-arrest technique; only later did I learn that I had learned and practiced a faulty method. My heavy backpack had weighed me down and contributed to my fall, but it ultimately may have saved my life by absorbing some impact when I landed on my back. (*Source: Don Sarver.*)

SKIERS AND SNOWBOARDERS IN RAINIER CREVASSES: *Three riders fell into crevasses on various Rainier glaciers, and one of them was killed.*

On May 27, a 24-year-old woman in a party of three that had summited earlier that day fell deep into a crevasse at 12,300 feet on the Winthrop Glacier. Rangers flew to Liberty Saddle, downclimbed to the crevasse, and raised the injured but responsive woman about 100 feet to escape the crevasse. The skier was short-hauled off the mountain by helicopter the next morning.

On July 16, a 42-year-old skier had summited Rainier by the Emmons Glacier route with two companions. During the descent, he fell into a crevasse at 12,900 feet. Rangers helicoptered to the summit and downclimbed to the scene, where they lowered about 150 feet into the crevasse and discovered the skier had passed away.

On September 22, a snowboarder fell 30 feet into a crevasse on the Inter Glacier, but despite some injuries, he and his partner were able to self-rescue and descend to the trailhead.

FALL ON SNOW | Fatigue, Poor Snow Conditions
Mt. Adams, North Cleaver

On July 7, my climbing partner (Hayley Dukatz, 31) and I set off from high camp for a run at the Adams Glacier on the north side of Mt. Adams. We had both climbed the mountain several times via other technical and nontechnical routes. A strong, warm wind blew throughout the night, so while the sky was clear, the snow did not firm up at all.

After an uneventful ascent, we began our descent from the summit by the North Cleaver Route: a nontechnical, scree-covered ridge that runs adjacent to the Adams Glacier. Around 9,000 feet, we encountered a brief snow traverse. My partner slipped on the soft, slick snow, and I promptly fell too. Tired and now angry, I stepped onto the exposed ridge, following in Hayley's path. One of her footsteps collapsed and I started to slide. I immediately went into self-arrest, and my axe stuck briefly before the pick popped out and I was off to the races.

The slope was steep and fairly uniform but for one little opening about halfway down, which I may have hit with the tip of my ice axe. My partner said I caught air. About 300 feet below, I landed in a crevasse/moat and was knocked unconscious.

I came to quickly and immediately donned layers. I saw blood in my saliva and felt intense pain in my right posterior ribs, and so I decided to activate my satellite messenger's SOS.

I crawled out of the moat and began to laboriously descend the Lava Glacier, contouring the ridgeline we'd been following. I wasn't able to take in full breaths of air, and each step compounded the effort. Eventually, I was able to put my pack back on and negotiate some mid-5th-class terrain to regain the ridge, at which point my partner and I met up.

We evaluated my injuries and decided to ask for a rescue, given that camp was still 2,000 feet below us, with a five-mile hike out after that, the sun was setting, and we had little remaining food. A helicopter airlifted my partner and me off the mountain. The hospital confirmed a comminuted mandibular fracture (jaw fracture) and I received surgery 10 days later.

ANALYSIS
The snow conditions were less than ideal, but that we knew from the first step. We post-holed up many sections of the Adams Glacier and the icefall. As the day warmed and the sun shone, the snow turned from soft to slushy. These conditions were not the cause of the accident, but they introduced time pressure by greatly increasing our climbing time.

As we descended, my fatigue was on full display as I slipped and fell several times on the abundant scree. By the time we'd encountered the fateful traverse, the snow quality was very soft and slick. Falling into the snow just before the exposed section caused me to lose what little remained of my focus, and thus I failed to evaluate my footing before committing my full weight. I was lucky to sustain only the injuries that I did, and to have external assistance available to me.

Finally, I believe that pressure in the mountains exacerbates personality traits—having an accident like this is not necessarily one and done. The core issue of charging ahead feverishly when irritation takes root rather than staying cautious, alert, and careful must be addressed. (*Source: Alexander Vasarab, 28.*)

WEST VIRGINIA

GROUND FALL | Protection Pulled Out, No Helmet
New River Gorge, Endless Wall, Fantasy Area

On June 25, at approximately 3:25 p.m., a male climber (age 27) fell while leading Black and Tan, a 5.10a trad line in the Fantasy area of Endless Wall. He was approximately 40 feet up the route and took a short fall onto his fourth protection piece, a number 0.3 Camalot, which pulled out. The resulting tug on the rope apparently levered out his third protection piece, a number 2 Wild Country nut, before he weighted it, and the next pieces down were too low to keep him from hitting the ground. The climber's legs impacted a less than vertical area on the lower part of the climb, upending him, and his head struck a rock on the ground. The belayer, who was using an ATC-style device, said that the rope never came taut before impact due to the slack in the system created from the pulled pieces of gear.

NPS rangers and rescue personnel responded to the accident and stabilized the patient, who eventually was evacuated by helicopter. A follow-up interview with the belayer by NPS personnel revealed that the climber had suffered lacerations to his head, a concussion, a collapsed lung, and a number of fractured ribs. He was not wearing a helmet. (*Source: National Park Service IMARS incident report and eyewitness Pat Goodman.*)

ANALYSIS

The pulled cam and nut were in good working order. Careful placement of gear, especially when using small cams, is necessary to prevent dangerous falls. It's often wise to place multiple pieces close together if the individual placements aren't ideal. Care also must be taken to extend nut placements appropriately; a longer sling on this nut might have prevented it from levering out. Also, a helmet might have prevented or mitigated the mild brain injury. (*Source: The Editors.*)

RAPPEL ERROR | Uneven Ropes, No Stopper Knots
New River Gorge, Junkyard

At approximately 5:30 p.m. on March 25, a 25-year-old male climber set up a rappel at the bolted anchors of Frigidator Crack (5.10b) and began to descend. Approximately halfway down, the climber rappelled off one of the strands of his 60-meter rope and fell 30 to 40 feet to the ground. The climber suffered numerous injuries, including head trauma (he was not wearing a helmet), and was flown to Charleston Area Medical Center. (*Source: National Park Service IMARS incident report.*)

ANALYSIS

Frigidator Crack is located between the main wall of Junkyard and a large detached flake that creates a narrow cave. The anchors for this route are easily accessible from the top of the cliff and are often used by climbers and guides to rappel. While the rappel is not difficult to set up, the bottom of the cave can be difficult to see in low light conditions, and this likely contributed to the climber's uneven rope ends.

If a rope does not have an accurate midpoint marker, climbers should ask people below if both ends are on the ground before committing to a rappel. When this isn't an option, the two rope ends should be lowered together so you can be certain that the midpoint is at the anchor. Finally, this is yet another example of the val-

The view down from the anchors above Frigidator Crack. The dark cave can make it hard to see the rope ends when setting up a rappel. *R. Bryan Simon*

ue of stopper knots in both ends of rappel ropes. Although some climbers may feel that placing stopper knots is unnecessary in single-pitch terrain, doing so in this instance likely would have prevented the accident. (*Source: The Editors.*)

RAPPEL ERROR | Uneven Ropes, No Stopper Knots
New River Gorge, Endless Wall, Fern Point

At 7:15 p.m. on July 15, a 22-year-old male climber rappelled off one of the ends of his rope while descending from S'more Energy (5.11c) on the Party Buttress. He fell approximately 40 feet and landed primarily on his feet, suffering multiple injuries. He was treated and evacuated by NPS rangers and local rescue personnel, and then transported by ambulance and helicopter to a nearby medical center. (*Source: National Park Service IMARS incident report.*)

ANALYSIS
The climber noted in an interview with NPS rangers that his party had lowered from the same anchors prior to the accident, verifying that their rope was long enough for the rappel. He also noted that he had used an autoblock backup for this rappel, but that he had not confirmed that the rope ends were on the ground and had not tied stopper knots in both strands. Either of these precautions would have prevented this accident. (*Source: The Editors.*)

LEADER FALL ONTO LEDGE | Inexperience
New River Gorge, Bubba City, Tattoo Wall

On the morning of October 28, with rain forecasted to begin by midday, my girl-friend, Liza Mindemann (age 33), and I (age 39) decided to get an early start on the third day of a two-week climbing road trip. We'd been together not even two months, and climbing is very much part of our relationship. In fact, we met at the Gunks, and since then I'd been teaching her to lead trad. She'd led up to 5.7 at the Gunks and followed a few 5.10s.

Walking down the approach trail to Tattoo Wall, I suggested she jump on Mrs. Field's Follies (5.8 sport) first thing. The day before, she had led Geisha Girl (5.8), her first ever sport lead, with no problems. She also had tried the adjacent Mrs. Field's, one of the longest moderates at the New. However, it was the end of the day, she was spent, and she couldn't get past the roof at the eighth bolt.

When we arrived, I announced (all too eagerly) that "we had an appointment with Mrs. Fields." With no actual discussion but only a kind of acquiescence to my more dominant energy–plus a certain rationality in both of us warming up on the 5.8–it was decided that Liza would try Mrs. Field's Follies right away. In retrospect, I believe this was the single most important factor in the subsequent accident.

Liza led past the first few bolts with no outward issues, but at the first crux, on a slabby section with potential for smacking the ledge below, she grabbed a bolt with her finger and screamed in frustration, "I just cheated!" She continued up the relatively easier sections above, still exhibiting nervousness and not breathing smoothly, until she reached the eighth bolt, where she had lowered off the day before. She stepped up to the roof to clip, backed down, and on the second attempt she pulled the roof successfully. She was psyched. However, she was unable to find a good position to clip the next bolt above the roof. She soon peeled off and impacted a ledge below. With pain in her right foot, she lowered to the base.

Once on the ground, it was clear Liza could not stand on her right foot and it was most likely broken. After cleaning the route with Liza belaying in relative calm (amazingly), I set her up with a phone and jacket to sit on and ran to the car to ditch the pack and grab some duct tape. We rigged a splint and I piggybacked her most of the way back to the car. At the local urgent-care facility, the physician's assistant diagnosed her with a possible comminuted fracture to the calcaneus and talus, later confirmed by CT scans at the local hospital. Fortunately, surgery was not required. (*Source: Sam Janis.*)

ANALYSIS

On easier climbs at the New River Gorge (and elsewhere), ledge falls are often a hazard for the leader. Mrs. Field's Follies is 100 feet tall, and given the amount of rope out at that point, rope stretch was a likely contributor to the ledge fall.

The climber probably best identified the causes of the accident when she stated, "Being relatively new to the sport, I find one of my biggest frustrations comes from the inconsistency in my climbing, knowing I can do something but...letting the mental game overthrow my ability to remain present in the climb. Thinking I was only a few moves away from the top, I started up somewhat carelessly, looking for favorable hands, not finding them, but moving up anyways, thinking better handholds would be revealed and essentially forgetting my feet." Many new climbers face similar challenges. (*Source: Sam Janis, Liza Mindemann, and the Editors.*)

FERN BUTTRESS LEDGE FALL: *On June 3, a male climber (age unknown) attempted to lead Ritz Cracker (5.9 trad). According to a National Park Service report, the climber fell above his last piece of gear and impacted the prominent ledge about halfway up the route, injuring an ankle. While additional details regarding the fall were not available, adequate protection and an attentive belay are essential above ledges and other terrain where a fall could result in injury. (Source: The Editors.)*

LOWERING VS. RAPPELLING AT THE NEW

While no single anchor-cleaning tactic can account for every situation, the New River Alliance of Climbers (NRAC, the climber non-profit that maintains and replaces anchors in the area) prefers that you *lower* when climbing at the New River Gorge. NRAC's stance is that lowering is faster and more efficient at crowded crags and is often less dangerous than rappelling. Both of the climbing fatalities at the New and numerous accidents every year are the result of rigging or conducting rappels incorrectly. NRAC sees no reason to unnecessarily introduce one of the most dangerous aspects of multi-pitch climbing into single-pitch cragging. Anchors can be replaced, but lives cannot.

Climbers who go single-pitch cragging should familiarize themselves with safe cleaning practices that never take them off belay. (See "Cleaning an Anchor in Single Pitch Climbing" at the AAC website for one good method.) For more information about NRAC, visit www.newriverclimbing.net.

WYOMING

SKI MOUNTAINEERING | Off-Route, Unable to Self-Arrest
Grand Teton National Park, South Teton

On February 16, at 11:10 a.m., park dispatch received a call that a skier had fallen down the Amora Vida Couloir on the south side of South Teton. Ranger Scott Guenther assumed incident command (IC) and spoke with the reporting party. She indicated that their party was "just at the entrance" [on top of] the Amora Vida Couloir, that one of her ski partners had fallen, and that he was not responding to calls via the hand-held radios they were carrying. She stated that they were a party of three females and one male, and that the male had fallen. She also said they would try to descend to him, if possible. Guenther asked them to be very careful and to descend only if it could be done safely.

South Teton from the air. Red line: Approximate ski route. (1) Entrance to Amora Vida Couloir, partially hidden on left. (2) Approximate fall site. *NPS Photo*

Guenther called for a Teton County SAR helicopter. At 12:18 p.m., he spoke again to the reporting party, who indicated they had climbed back uphill and had determined they were not actually in the Amora Vida Couloir but instead had entered a different couloir on the southeast face of the South Teton. They also said that they would hold in place rather than ascend further, as the snow was warming and becoming potentially unstable.

The helicopter was en route to the scene at 12:36 p.m. Rescuers located the party and then searched downhill from their location, soon spotting the victim. He appeared to be motionless and had fallen a distance later estimated to be approximately 1,200 vertical feet. At 1 p.m., the helicopter landed in Avalanche Canyon and dropped off three rescuers, who skied and climbed to the victim, arriving at 1:40 p.m. The skier was determined to be deceased.

Later that afternoon, the victim was extracted by helicopter long line. Staying in contact with the IC throughout the afternoon and evening, the three remaining members of the party reclimbed South Teton, arriving on the summit at approximately 7 p.m., and then descended Garnet Canyon, reaching the Taggart Lake Trailhead at about 10:30 p.m.

ANALYSIS

The partners and friend of the victim [John "Jack" Fields, 26] described him as an expert skier. Since arriving in the area about two months prior, he had skied a number of technical descents in the Teton Range. His partners and he would all be considered to have the requisite skill and experience to ski the Amora Vida Couloir.

The victim's partners described the skiing conditions prior to the accident as pretty good. They practiced safe technique, skiing one at a time between safe areas. At one point, the question of whether they were on the right route came up; however, the subject, who had the most route information, made the decision to start down the couloir where the accident occurred. He also decided to keep his skis on his feet while navigating a short narrow section that required his tips and tails to be touching the rock. Unfortunately, the heel piece of his Dynafit bindings released. (The skis were not recovered, so the binding description came from his partners). Since his toe piece did not release, it is presumed that he had it in the upright, or locked, position. It is not uncommon for ski mountaineers to descend steep, committing terrain with the toe piece locked to prevent inadvertent release.

Witness statements indicate that the subject did not appear tense or scared even after the heel piece released, and he worked to position himself to click back into his binding. When he started to slide, he attempted to self-arrest using his Whippet (ski-pole self-arrest grip). However, the snow was too soft for the Whippet to gain any purchase. Unfortunately, in this type of high-consequence terrain, there is very little margin for error or equipment failure. (*Source: National Park Service Search and Rescue Report.*)

FALL ON SNOW | Not Wearing Crampons, Failure to Self-Arrest
Grand Teton National Park, Disappointment Peak

On the morning of June 19, two climbers began ascending the Spoon Couloir of Disappointment Peak. The day was sunny and warm. Once the climbers reached the top of the couloir, they decided against continuing to the summit and instead planned to descend via the "Chockstone Couloir" (fourth class and steep snow) on the southeast ridge of Disappointment Peak.

At 1:30 p.m., at approximately 10,300 feet, one of the climbers (male, 68) slipped on snow and fell approximately 400 feet, dropping over a cliff along the way. He was not wearing crampons. Hikers who witnessed the fall reported the accident; they said the subject was moaning and blowing a whistle, and that they were unable to reach his location.

Ranger Marty Vidak, on patrol in the area, descended from near the summit of Disappointment Peak and reached the injured climber at 2:45 p.m., finding him in steep terrain approximately 300 vertical feet above Amphitheater Lake. He was treated and air evacuated to St. John's Hospital, where he was found to have suffered flail chest, a thoracic cavity bleed, fractures of the T7 and L4 vertebrae, a fractured patella, and shoulder trauma. His partner, with the assistance of another climber, descended unharmed. (*Source: National Park Service Search and Rescue Report.*)

ANALYSIS
Wearing crampons and effectively utilizing an ice axe to self-arrest could have prevented this accident. The two climbers had experience on steep snow and were outfitted with boots, ice axes, crampons, helmets, and other appropriate equipment. The snow was firm at the site of the fall, and the climbers may have been

lulled into a false sense of security after ascending the Spoon Couloir in softer snow, failing to anticipate the icier conditions on the descent. The patient's helmet was damaged during the fall, suggesting it might have prevented another serious injury. (*Source: The Editors.*)

STRANDED | Off-Route, Benighted
Grand Teton National Park, Mt. Moran

On August 8, at approximately 2 a.m., ranger Chris Harder was notified that a climbing party was stuck on the CMC Route of Mt. Moran. The two climbers (male, ages 58 and 35) had begun their climb from the CMC Camp (about 2,600 feet below the summit) at 5 a.m. Difficulty with route-finding and multiple episodes of stuck ropes and gear resulted in a late summit (4:30 p.m.). After a brief rest, the two began descending and encountered more route-finding difficulties, challenging downclimbing, and stuck rappel ropes. They continued to descend after dark and ultimately got off-route onto the lower portion of the Black Dike, skier's left of the proper route. After contacting the park and confirming that neither was injured, the two were advised that a rescue would be launched the following morning.

No-fall terrain and few landmarks make the upper CMC Route no place to be racing darkness. The Black Dike is at far left. *Michael Schneiter*

Early on August 9, a helicopter crew quickly found the pair on a large ledge on the Black Dike. Two rangers began climbing to their location, as weather prevented the helicopter from reaching the climbers. In the early afternoon, however, the weather cleared and ranger Phil Edmonds was short-hauled to the ledge. He placed both climbers in screamer suits, and all three were short-hauled to Lupine Meadows. (*Source: National Park Service Search and Rescue Report.*)

ANALYSIS
Route-finding can be difficult in the Tetons due to the complex and sometimes amorphous terrain. However, detailed descriptions and photos of this route are available in print and online; consider carrying several versions to compare in case of difficulties. Climber comments in online route descriptions often provide more information.

Various difficulties caused this team to reach the summit very late in the day, and then further slowed them during the descent. Setting a turnaround time before starting for a summit—and sticking to it—will minimize exposure to environmental hazards (dangerously warm snow, lightning) and allow adequate time to descend before nightfall. (*Source: The Editors.*)

STRANDED | Route-Finding Errors, Inadequate Clothing
Grand Teton National Park, Grand Traverse

On the afternoon of August 11, a 30-year-old male, Climber 1, and 23-year-old female, Climber 2, began an attempt on the Grand Traverse, a complex and challenging route linking ten Teton summits. Climber 1 had been climbing for about eight years, primarily bouldering and sport climbing, with minimal traditional and alpine climbing experience. In the Tetons, he had done the complete Exum Ridge on the Grand Teton. Climber 2 had been climbing for 10 years, with a strong sport climbing resumé but limited traditional climbing experience and no alpine experience. This was her first visit to the Tetons.

For this climb they brought standard rock climbing equipment, climbing shoes, and a 70-meter rope. Overnight gear included a tent, two lightweight sleeping bags, and food for four days and three nights. Personal gear included warm insulating layers and trail running shoes. Neither of them brought a rain jacket or rain pants.

In three days they climbed over Teewinot and Mt. Owen and made it to the Grandstand at the base of the north ridge of the Grand. They were moving much slower than expected due to the complexity of route-finding and the constant exposed climbing in unfamiliar terrain. They realized that they could not complete the Grand Traverse but were hoping to finish their trip on the fourth day by climbing the north ridge of the Grand Teton, descending the Owen-Spalding Route, and then walking down from the Lower Saddle.

It rained overnight, and they woke to light rain and poor visibility. They decided to attempt the north ridge (the crux of the Grand Traverse, 5.8 and approximately 10 pitches) despite the poor weather, because, in their minds, it was the only way off the mountain. Route-finding was difficult due to limited visibility, and the climbing was increasingly difficult amid rain and snow showers. They were losing dexterity in their fingers and toes, and at one point, Climber 1 took an estimated 40-foot fall but was able to complete the pitch. Higher on the route, snowfall began increasing. On August 14, at approximately 4:30 p.m., Climber 1 called the Teton dispatch center and was transferred to SAR coordinator Gordon Fletcher.

Fletcher had a brief discussion with the distressed party, attempting to determine their location in relation to the Second Ledge, which is an exit to the Upper Saddle. They were unaware if they had passed or had yet to arrive at Second Ledge. Ranger Fletcher explained that, due to current weather conditions, it was unlikely that rescue personnel could get to them that night and they would need to find a way to stay as comfortable as they could until morning.

Rangers at the Lower Saddle reported light snow and strong winds, with accumulating snow at the Upper Saddle. At 6:20 p.m., rangers Phil Edmonds and Vic Zeilman began to ascend toward the Upper Saddle with climbing and rescue gear, with the idea of crossing the Second Ledge to see if they could make contact with the distressed climbers. However, the climbing conditions were too hazardous and they returned to the Lower Saddle. The climbers reported they were able to rappel to a ledge and get in a tent, and they spent the night there.

On the morning of August 15, the climbers were still wet and cold, but the clouds had lifted, the sun was coming out, and they could see the Grandstand an estimated 300 feet below them. Two rappels brought them back to the Grandstand,

at 12,600 feet, where they called ranger Fletcher again to report their location. Due to the length and challenge of the coming descent and the climbers' current physical and mental condition, it was determined that it would be best if they were extracted from the Grandstand. By midday, after several helicopter flights, rangers successfully short-hauled both climbers from the Grandstand to Lupine Meadows. (*Source: National Park Service Search and Rescue Report.*)

The Cathedral Traverse from near the top of Teewinot. (A) Grand Teton. (B) The Grandstand. (C) Mt. Owen. (D) Peak 11,840'. The Koven Route (see p.108) gains the snowfields on Owen from the left. *Rolando Garibotti*

ANALYSIS

The Grand Traverse is easy to underestimate because of its modest technical grade. Ample experience with Tetons climbing and alpine route-finding should be a prerequisite to attempting this linkup, and reconnaissance of key sections, including planning for escape routes, will help ensure success. Rain gear is essential for any climb in the Tetons, no matter how good the forecast. (*Source: The Editors.*)

RAPPEL ERROR | Uneven Ropes
Grand Teton National Park, Cathedral Traverse, Peak 11,840'

On August 25, at 10:15 a.m., Grand Teton SAR coordinator Drew Hardesty was contacted by Exum guide Joe Stern, who reported that he had found a deceased solo climber at the base of the rappels on the southwest side of Peak 11,840', a summit between Teewinot and Mt. Owen, often traversed as part of the Cathedral Traverse or Grand Traverse. At 12:15 p.m., rangers were flown to Peak 11,840', rappelled to the deceased climber, and arranged to have his body flown off the mountain. The climber was later identified as Alexander Kenan (24) from North Carolina.

From photos and social media posts by the deceased, it was determined that he had fallen on the morning of August 22, likely between 7:30 and 9 a.m. In their investigation, rangers determined he had fallen approximately 65 feet from the final rappel on the southwest face of Peak 11,840', after rappelling off the end of his rope. A locking carabiner was found attached to the belay loop on the climber's harness and clipped to a tube-style rappel device, with the screw gate locked. A 60-meter rope (estimated to be 8mm to 9mm in diameter, with a faded middle mark) was properly loaded in the rappel device's right slot. The left slot was empty. Both the carabiner and rappel device were structurally intact, the rope showed no signs of damage or wear, and a prusik was on the subject's harness but not rigged to be used as a backup.

One end of the rope had a barrel knot tied in it approximately seven inches from the end, while the other end of the rope was unknotted. The knotted end of the rope came out of the brake-hand side of the rappel device and extended 46 feet below. This information (combined with burns on the decedent's left hand, which was likely his upper stabilization hand during the rappel) suggests that the ends of the rope were uneven during the rappel and that he rappelled off one end of the rope. (*Source: National Park Service Search and Rescue Report.*)

ANALYSIS

This particular rappel transitions from blockier terrain to a final bulge that would have made the ends of the rope difficult to see from above. The climber likely would not have been able to observe the disparity in rope lengths until very shortly before his fall.

One of two scenarios likely occurred. One, the victim tied stopper knots in both ends of the rope, but one knot perhaps came undone during the rappel. The other scenario is that, while stationed at his last rappel anchor, he fed rope through the anchor, tied a stopper knot in that end of the rope, and fed it down the cliff as he pulled the rope from the previous rappel. In this scenario, he did not put a knot in the end that fell from above and did not pull the rope ends up to ensure they were even. Either way, when he reached the unknotted end, approximately 75 feet below the anchor, the rope end would have pulled through his device and he would have fallen about 25 feet and then tumbled another 40 feet down ledge-filled terrain.

Three 100-foot rappels descend Peak 11,840'. *Rolando Garibotti*

When rigging rappels where the rope ends are not visible below, be sure the rope's middle mark is centered at the anchor. If the rope is not marked (or if there is any chance the rope has been cut so the middle mark is incorrect), lower the two ends together to ensure they remain even. Either way, place stopper knots in both ends and use a friction-hitch backup. (*Source: National Park Service Search and Rescue Report and the Editors.*)

ROCKFALL ON APPROACH

Garnet Canyon

On the morning of August 26, rangers received a call from a woman saying that one of her climbing partners was trapped under large boulders that had rolled over her in the Lower South Fork of Garnet Canyon. The party of three had been avoiding snow on the second rise of the canyon, at approximately 10,100 feet, when the reporting party knocked down loose rocks that struck her partner (female, age 24), who was 40 feet below. The climbers had removed one boulder from the patient's chest, but her legs were trapped by another large rock. She had a bleeding head injury and difficulty breathing.

Rangers responded by helicopter, removed the boulder (estimated at 100 pounds and 14 inches in diameter), and freed the patient. The patient was short-hauled from the scene. (*Source: National Park Service Search and Rescue Report.*)

ANALYSIS

Although this was not a climbing accident, per se, the hazards of loose talus and rock-filled ledges are encountered in many climbing environments. All members of a party should take great care to avoid knocking off loose rocks or starting slides and immediately yell "Rock!" if something does fall. If possible, travel on a diagonal path so one climber is not directly beneath the other. It's usually best to stay close together on open slopes—for better communication and to avoid rockfall before it gains dangerous and unpredictable momentum—but move one at a time through gullies or other constricted areas.

Finally, consider donning your helmet for approaches through steep talus or scree and leaving it on for the full descent. You have to carry it anyway—it might as well be doing some good. (*Source: The Editors.*)

FALL ON SNOW | Failure to Self-Arrest, Loss of Equipment
Grand Teton National Park, Mt. Owen

On August 26, at 12:30 p.m., ranger Jim Springer received a cell phone call from two climbers attempting the Koven Route on Mt. Owen. (A second pair in the same party was attempting the route separately.) According to the caller, the climbers were attempting to traverse around to the south side of the summit when the one of them (female, age 23) slipped on snow and began sliding. She was unable to self-arrest and then lost her ice axe. She impacted a rock ledge at the base of the snowfield, injuring her left ankle.

After speaking with ranger Springer, the two climbers and their friends decided to attempt their own rescue by descending the Koven Couloir to their camp on the Teton Glacier. It took approximately six hours to rappel and downclimb the couloir. Back at their camp, the group of four decided to call again for help. At 8:30 p.m., one of them hiked to Amphitheater Lake to get cell service and called Springer, who advised them to be prepared for evacuation in the morning. The patient and her partner were flown to Lupine Meadows the next day. (*Source: National Park Service Search and Rescue Report.*)

ANALYSIS

Nearly every year, climbers are injured or killed due to falls on snow in the Tetons, compounded by their inability to self-arrest. Prevention of falls on snow and ice begins with assessing snow conditions and using the appropriate boots and equipment, as well as good footwork on snow of varying angles and proper use of an ice axe. Practice self-arrest before entering terrain with serious consequences. "Danger Zones: The Grand Teton" (*Accidents* 2016) and "Know the Ropes: Snow Climbing" (*Accidents* 2014) are good basic references; both articles are available online. Field training with a guide or skilled mentor is the best way to learn. (*Source: The Editors.*)

GRAND TETON FALLS: *On August 18, at around 4:15 p.m., rangers were notified that a climber had sustained traumatic injuries in an unroped fall while descending about 200 feet below the summit of the Grand. The climber, one of four brothers climbing together, had tumbled headfirst approximately 20 feet over steep rock. He was not wearing a helmet. Rangers were flown to the scene about two hours later. After the patient's injuries were stabilized, he was short-hauled from the accident site and transferred to an air ambulance at Lupine Meadows.*

On August 28, a climber fell 15 to 20 feet on the first pitch of the Lower Exum Ridge, likely breaking his foot and possibly his tailbone. The climber had placed protection about 20 feet above the belayer, moved up and slightly off-route to the left, and attempted unsuccessfully to place more protection. He then attempted to pull through a roof without pro and fell, impacting a ledge. The belayer lowered him, and the two, who had met online and had only climbed together once before, managed to descend several hundred feet of fourth class to reach a point where, a few hours later, the patient could be short-hauled from the scene. (Source: National Park Service Search and Rescue Reports.)

FATAL FALL | Unroped Scrambling During Descent
Wind River Range, Steeple Peak

On Monday, August 28, Michael Sullivan, 54, fell to his death while descending from Steeple Peak. Sullivan and his climbing partner had done other ascents earlier that week in the Cirque of the Towers area. On August 28 they had reached the summit of Steeple Peak in the Deep Lake cirque and were on their way down the standard south ridge descent. While scrambling unroped between the first and second rappel stations, Sullivan lost his footing and fell hundreds of feet. His partner descended on her own and hiked until she met a party with a satellite phone and called for help. (*Source: Sublette County Sheriff's Office.*)

ANALYSIS
The victim was an experienced mountaineer, with numerous ascents of alpine climbs in the United States and elsewhere. The descent from Steeple involves a series of rappels with walking and scrambling between them. It's not known exactly where or why the victim stumbled, but scrambling is the normal way to move between rappel stations on this descent. (*Source: The Editors.*)

DEVILS TOWER FATALITY: *On the afternoon of June 2, a 38-year-old man fell while leading the Sundance Route (5.7) and sustained fatal head injuries. He was wearing a helmet. Further details were not available. The last climbing fatality at Devils Tower was in 2003.*

Steeple Peak (left) in the Wind River Range. The descent route is near Steeple's right skyline.
Garrett Harmsen

CANADA

Unless otherwise noted, the narratives in the Canada section are drawn from national and regional park reports. Analyses were provided by park rangers and Robert Chisnall of the Alpine Club of Canada.

MT. LOGAN RESCUES
Yukon Territory, Kluane National Park

In April, a party of three climbers attempting the east ridge of Mt. Logan required evacuation from approximately 4,800 meters (15,748 feet). One of the members was experiencing symptoms of high altitude cerebral edema (HACE).

In early May, a female solo climber, nine days into a traverse of Logan, was unable to continue up the east ridge as a result of a severe earthquake, followed by a prolonged storm. The terrain above and below her became unstable. After three days of waiting out the storm, she was evacuated from 3,700 meters (12,139 feet).

In late May a climber injured his knee while skiing back from Prospector's Peak on the King Trench route of Mt. Logan and was unable to continue. A rescue party was able to land at approximately 4,700 meters (15,419 feet) the same day and evacuate the climber and his guide.

ANALYSIS
All of these incidents underscore the value of having a self-rescue plan, the ability and preparedness to wait for assistance if self-rescue is not an option, and effective means of communications with rescuers. (*Source: Scott Stewart, Visitor Safety Coordinator, Kluane National Park and Reserve.*)

FALL ON ROCK | Inadequate Protection, Inexperience
British Columbia, Squamish, Stawamus Chief

My climbing partner, Scott, and I were first responders to an accident high on the Chief on September 7. We had climbed Rock On and planned to continue up the Squamish Buttress (mostly 5.6 with one 5.10c pitch; about six more pitches). At the top of Rock On, we met two climbers (Franz and Mitch, both in their early 20s), who had just finished Calculus Crack (5.8). They too intended to finish via the Squamish Buttress. We played rock-paper-scissors to see who went first, and they won the game and started climbing.

While I was leading the second-to-last and crux pitch, I heard what I thought was a substantial rockfall, then saw a body pendulum toward me, skipping and spinning off the wall, upside down. The climber stopped falling about 30 feet to my left, unconscious, very bloody, and still upside down. It was Mitch. He appeared to be dead for about one minute. I called down to Scott, my partner, to make sure he was okay, then quickly plugged in an anchor. Scott yelled up to take it slow and not to jeopardize our safety. It was a good reminder. During this communication, Mitch came back to consciousness with one enormous, gasping breath. He was reasonably alert and able to follow commands, but severely concussed. For the next hour, he would ask questions about where the blood came from and where he was.

The sheath of their rope was ripped clean for about 40 feet, and the rope showed core damage. We quickly formulated a plan for me to swing over to Mitch, clip him into me, and then Scott would lower both of us about 30 feet to his belay ledge from the temporary anchor I had built. Mitch's belayer, Franz, yelled down that he was still belaying Mitch with a Grigri and that he would be able to lower him as well.

Once down, we immobilized Mitch at the base of the crux pitch on a huge ledge. There was a lot of blood, but this was most likely from his nose; there were no open wounds on his head. We called for a rescue, and Mitch was airlifted off the Chief within two hours of the accident. We finished the climb as a team of three and walked down with Franz. Mitch survived with a serious concussion.

Helicopter rescue from Squamish Buttress. *Peter Morgan*

ANALYSIS

Mitch was leading the last pitch (5.6) when he fell. He had placed two small C3 cams right next to each other in a poor flaring seam, and both cams pulled out. He fell about 50 vertical feet and also pendulumed about 50 feet. Franz was flipped upside down, and I think he might have lost control of the belay if he had been using a tube-style device instead of a Grigri. I don't think Mitch would have survived if he had not been wearing a helmet. Both climbers were new to traditional, multi-pitch routes, and my partner and I observed that neither seemed to have solid technical skills.

On a separate note, it's a good idea to leave your car keys hidden near your car. Franz's shoes (and car keys) were in the backpack that fell off Mitch while he was upside down, and after descending the Chief in bare feet, he was somewhat stranded. (*Source: Peter Morgan.*)

LOWERING ERROR | No Stopper Knot
British Columbia, Squamish, Shannon Falls

On June 27 my climbing partner and I witnessed an accident on Cardhu Crack (one pitch, 5.8) in the Shannon Falls area. After successfully completing the climb, the leader was being lowered. When she was about four meters above the ground, the belayer's end of the rope went through her device and the leader fell to the ground. The belayer tried to catch the leader and was badly scraped and bruised in the process.

Miraculously, everyone was able to walk away from the incident without any broken limbs. Both persons were wearing their helmets, and judging by a dent in the climber's helmet, it probably saved her from a much more severe injury.

ANALYSIS

The climbers (both in their 20s) said they had a 70-meter rope, which they believed to be long enough to lower from this route. However, guidebook descriptions should not be trusted blindly, and ropes often shrink with age and use. Although lowering from this route is possible with a 70-meter rope, care must be taken with the location of the belayer and the climber's landing. More to the point, tying a stopper knot at the end of the rope or tying in the belayer would have prevented this accident. (*Source: Yannick Gingras.*)

BELAYER PULLED INTO WALL | No Ground Anchor
British Columbia, Vancouver Island, Nanaimo

On October 8, a 24-year-old woman caught her climbing partner's fall at the Lower Deck of the Sunnyside climbing area. (Whether the climber was leading or top-roping was not clear from reports.) The belayer was pulled forward, slamming into rock and seriously injuring her knee. Rescuers hauled her to the top of the cliff in a litter and transported her to the hospital. (*Source: Times Colonist newspaper, Victoria, BC.*)

ANALYSIS

Climbers should be mindful of several issues when belaying heavier leaders from the ground. If the climber weighs substantially more than the belayer (50 percent or greater weight difference is a good guideline), the belayer should be appropriately anchored; however, be aware of rockfall danger to the belayer and the ability to communicate effectively with the climber. The belayer should be positioned as directly under the leader as the terrain and overhead hazards allow. Avoid belaying from perches on boulders, talus, or hillsides where the sudden force of a fall may cause the belayer to swing or be dragged across the ground. (*Source: The Editors.*)

AVALANCHE
British Columbia, Northern Selkirks

Our party of six attempted an abbreviated version of the North Selkirks ski traverse, starting on April 16. On Friday, April 21, we left the Great Cairn (Ben Ferris) hut for the Guardsman Glacier and the summit of the Footstool, adjacent to Mt. Sir Sandford. We summited the Footstool on skis around noon, then waited out some cloudy weather for about an hour. From the col east of the summit of Footstool, we descended to the north from approximately 3,100 meters to roughly 2,850 meters on the Guardsman Glacier. At about 1:45 p.m. we decided to do another run adjacent to our ski tracks.

At approximately 2 p.m., while we were ascending our up-track, a natural, size 3 slab avalanche originating at about 3,000 meters on a northeast aspect caught three of the six members of our group. Two members were injured, requiring full

ESSENTIALS

AVALANCHE RESPONSE
PHYSIOLOGY, RESCUE, AND RESUSCITATION

By Dave Weber and Dr. Colin Grissom

This article outlines the causes of morbidity and mortality in avalanche incidents, as well as prudent and practical rescue steps and medical treatments, based on the 2017 Wilderness Medical Society *Practice Guidelines for Prevention and Management of Avalanche and Nonavalanche Snow Burial Accidents.*

Avalanche risk can be mitigated by recognizing and avoiding dangerous conditions such as steep terrain (>30°), inclement weather, and an unstable snowpack. Formal avalanche education and mentored experience in avalanche terrain are the best ways to gain the required skills.

If caught in an avalanche, the top priorities should be getting off the sliding snow surface and fighting to stay on top of the snow. If buried by an avalanche, one's companions are the best hope for survival.

PATHOPHYSIOLOGY

The outcome of an avalanche burial is influenced by several factors, including the length of time buried, whether the patient's airway is open, if there is an air pocket, how deep they were buried, and if they were injured. The majority (75%) of avalanche fatalities occur due to asphyxia (lack of oxygen); a smaller percentage (25%) occur from traumatic injuries; and a very small number of victims succumb to hypothermia.

Asphyxia is caused by inhaled snow blocking the airway, the rebreathing of exhaled air, or an ice mask that forms over the airway after burial. Given that a lack of oxygen causes such a great number of fatalities, efficient extrication is key to the patient's survival. European research suggests that if the patient is extricated within 15 minutes, the chance of survival is greater than 90%. If the time of extrication extends to 30 minutes, the chance of survival plummets to 30%.

The specific injuries that account for the 25% of avalanche deaths from trauma vary greatly. Most injuries are caused by collisions with trees or rocks or travel over cliffs.

Asphyxiation is more likely to kill an avalanche victim before core temperature decreases enough to cause death from severe hypothermia. However, it is important to consider hypothermia due to its detrimental effect on other medical/traumatic conditions. Once the patient is extricated from the insulating snow, core temperature can drop rapidly.

RESCUE

A systematic approach to avalanche rescue is of utmost importance. During an avalanche accident, rescuers should follow a rescue sequence, of which the key components are the establishment of leadership, a survey of the scene for risks to safety, a surface clue search, a transceiver search, a pinpoint (probe) search, strategic shoveling, medical care, patient evacuation, and the notification of emer-

RESCUE SEQUENCE

1 **Establish Leadership**

2 **Scene Safety Survey**

3 **Surface Search**

4 **Transceiver Search**

5 **Pinpoint/Probe Search**

6 **Strategic Shoveling**

7 **Medical Care**

8 **Evacuation**

Emergency services can be notified at any time, but don't delay initial response.

gency services. Depending on the number of available rescuers, individuals may be tasked with one or more elements of a rescue sequence.

RESUSCITATION AND FIELD TREATMENT

The International Commission for Alpine Rescue (ICAR) developed an avalanche victim resuscitation checklist aligned with the European Resuscitation Council (ERC) guidelines in 2010 and revised the original checklist in 2015. [*A flow chart outlining this checklist can be found by searching "ICAR resuscitation checklist." It also is included with this article at publications.americanalpineclub.org.*] The ICAR checklist was developed to provide a methodical approach to medical treatment in an austere winter environment.

Survivability is influenced by a range of factors, including airway patency (airway open and free of snow or ice), burial duration, injury severity, core temperature, and the patient's blood potassium level. Backcountry travelers with basic medical training should focus on basic life support (BLS).

It is important to note that no effective medical care can begin until the victim's head and chest are fully exposed. Once extricated, all avalanche victims should be assessed for airway patency, effective breathing, and circulation.

If known, the burial time can help to dictate care decisions. The first step in medical care is to triage avalanche victims into two groups: those buried for less than 60 minutes and those buried for greater than 60 minutes. If resources are limited, care should be focused on those buried less than 60 minutes.

If vital signs (respirations and a palpable pulse) are present, basic first aid should be administered as needed. This could include stopping any bleeding and splinting injuries. If vital signs are absent (no respirations and no pulse detected), rescuers should initiate cardiopulmonary resuscitation (CPR). For those buried more than 60 minutes, the same steps should be taken. In addition, the first responder should note if an ice mask was present in front of the victim's face, suggesting an air pocket under the snow that allowed the patient to keep breathing for some time.

If basic life support (BLS) treatment does not result in the return of spontaneous circulation (return of a palpable pulse) after 30 minutes of resuscitation, further CPR is not necessary as the chance of survival is minimal. Responders also may take into account obvious lethal trauma.

The ICAR guidelines for advanced (ALS) treatment of avalanche patients are typically reserved for trained providers with the necessary equipment. The checklist guides decision-making based on heart rhythm, core temperature, and potassium level. These steps are most appropriate in prehospital and hospital settings.

Dave Weber is a Denali mountaineering ranger and a flight paramedic for Intermountain Life Flight in Salt Lake City, Utah. Dr. Colin Grissom is a critical care physician for Intermountain Healthcare in Salt Lake City.

assistance, but were not buried. (One had a fractured left leg; the other had shoulder injuries.) One member was buried approximately one meter below the surface. He was recovered five to six minutes after burial and was mildly hypoxic but did not require resuscitation and was without injury. The other three members conducted the rescues and were able to summon help via VHF radio for further support and evacuation.

Mt. Sir Sandford and the Footstool, showing approximate avalanche extent. *John Scurlock*

ANALYSIS

The following factors were supportive of our decision to ski up and down this slope and then head up for another run. There was supportive snowpack, no avalanche activity had been observed that day or the preceding five days, and temperatures were stable. There was no deterioration to snow or ski quality consistent with rapid warming. The slope chosen to ski was very conservative: an angle of 20° or less. The slope that released was adjacent to our ski run and was quite steep (40° to 50°). This slope had been discussed as a potential risk during the initial ascent, and as a result the up-track and descent route were strategically made on the opposite side of the glacier. (This was the one factor that probably averted total disaster, because the main funnel of the avalanche missed us. Our group was caught in the leftmost fan of the slide, looking up.)

The following risk factors were unsupportive of our decision to ski a second run. The time of day, particularly in context with time of year (late April), were not ideal. The snowpack history was marked by a persistent weak layer deep in the snowpack (consisting of November facets and depth hoar). These conditions had set up a low-probability, high-consequence scenario through most of the mountain ranges of British Columbia, particularly throughout the East Columbia and Rocky Mountains. The steep slope adjacent to our ski run, although not impressive, held avalanche potential.

Our group discussed to a significant extent the pros and cons of undertaking or aborting a second run. Most of the factors above were brought up, although our confidence collectively had been bolstered regarding the persistent weak layer, based on our field observations. Some in the group were markedly reserved; others were motivated for a second run, including myself. After several minutes of indecision, the group collectively decided to go ahead.

In situations like the one described, where objective evidence of heightened risk is relatively low, subjective factors can play an important role in mitigating unnecessary risk and accident. Err toward the side of caution rather than confidence. A combination of fitness, motivational factors, and of course good weather caused our group, in particular myself, to overlook important human factors that should have weighed more heavily in the final decision. (*Source: Dr. David Urness, D.C.*)

FATAL SLIP ON ICE | Inadequate Equipment
British Columbia, Glacier National Park, Mt. Sir Donald

On July 15, TP and AM climbed the classic northwest ridge of Mt. Sir Donald. On the summit they met another pair of climbers and decided to descend together via the West Face Bypass route. As the group made their way down, they had to cross a few snow patches. Around 10:15 a.m., TP started to cross a snow patch, slipped, quickly lost control, and tumbled down the face out of view. AM activated a SPOT emergency communication device, and one of the other team members called 911.

A helicopter reconnaissance located the deceased climber, who had fallen

Parks Canada has created a detailed free guide to the descent options for Mt. Sir Donald. Search "Sir Donald descent guide" to download a copy. *Parks Canada*

about 240 meters. The three party members remaining above were evacuated from an elevation of 3,150 meters using a long-line, and the body was recovered the next morning.

ANALYSIS

The climber slipped and fell while crossing what had appeared to be a small snow patch–in fact it was just a few centimeters of soft snow over ice. He was wearing climbing approach shoes and did not have crampons or an ice axe. When snow patches are still visible on the West Face Bypass, it is advisable to carry an ice axe, crampons, and mountain boots for this descent to avoid potential falls. Alternatively, downclimbing and rappelling the northwest ridge would avoid having to deal with snow and ice on the bypass route.

STRANDED | Off Route
British Columbia, Yoho National Park, Chancellor Peak

Two climbers were attempting the west ridge of Chancellor Peak (3,266 meters) on July 24. They were expecting low fifth-class climbing and instead encountered what felt like 5.8 or 5.9, with little protection, on poor rock. The two simul-climbed an estimated 10 to 12 pitches along the ridge until they got to a steep section they could not safely climb. Their route description told them to look for a rightward traverse, but they could not find it. While looking for the correct path, they triggered a large rockfall, which unsettled them and made them feel they could not safely ascend or descend the route. They called Banff dispatch on their cell phone and requested a rescue. Both climbers were uninjured.

After some discussion with the Parks Canada rescue leader, it was determined the climbers could not be coached down safely. A helicopter and team were prepared for a technical sling rescue. The team had radio communication with the stranded party, and they were told to pack up all ropes, to minimize entanglement hazard. Two rescuers were flown in and picked off both climbers.

ANALYSIS

The Canadian Rockies are known for having some poor rock, which can make it difficult or impossible to find good protection or retreat anchors, especially on obscure or unpopular routes. It is important to keep descent options in mind and avoid climbing into a spot from which retreat or further ascent is impossible. The party had chosen this obscure route because it was described in a newly published guidebook. Climbers should use all available resources, including online trip reports, to be fully aware of what is involved in a planned route.

Location of stranded climbers on Chancellor Peak. *Parks Canada*

Although this climbing party climbed into a situation from which they could not move up or down, they were well equipped and prepared for the climb. They had two emergency communication devices, allowing them to speak to the rescue team on a radio as they flew overhead, which greatly facilitated the rescue and made it safer for everyone involved.

ROCKFALL

British Columbia, Yoho National Park, Mt. Hungabee

On September 3, a four-person team ascended the west ridge of Mt. Hungabee after a high bivouac the previous night. During the descent, one team member was struck on the helmet by a large rock while he was attached to an anchor. The climber had been leaning into the rock, face forward, to gain shelter from rockfall. When the impact occurred, the climber's face was slammed against the rock, resulting in a broken nose. The climbers were able to continue down to their bivouac, where they called for an evacuation.

It was extremely windy and a rescue helicopter failed several times to reach the party. After numerous tries, the rescue helicopter landed in the meadows below, and the climbing party was asked to begin descending on their own. Within 45 minutes the climbing team, with their injured climber, descended from the bivouac, crossed the glacier, and met the rescue team in the moraine below. The patient was evacuated from there.

ANALYSIS

Despite the patient sustaining a significant blow to the head, this party was able to descend under its own power—they could have simply walked out or else called from the meadows below, where helicopter access is much easier. Rescuers put themselves at significant risk to access injured patients. Consider self-evacuation when possible.

ROCKFALL | Poor Position
British Columbia, Takakkaw Falls

My girlfriend and I were climbing the standard Takakkaw Falls route (12 pitches, 5.6) on Labor Day weekend. When we arrived, two parties were already on the route: a guide and a young woman, and a less experienced party that had been knocking off loose rocks. I was in the middle of the ninth pitch, 15 meters below the top, when the inexperienced party started rappelling from above. Upon pulling their rope, they dislodged a toaster-size rock that fell about 40 meters before striking my thumb and inner thigh. The thumb was partially amputated and the distal phalange was shattered. My thigh had a large hematoma. We were able to rappel and then drive to Golden for medical aid.

ANALYSIS

Climbing a popular route known for rockfall on a holiday weekend was the first mistake our party made. Our second mistake was continuing up the route despite the rockfall hazard from the inexperienced party. The climbers that dislodged the

The popular 12-pitch Takakkaw Falls route is left of the waterfall. *Dougald MacDonald*

rock did not appear to yell "rope" before rappelling, nor "rock!" when they knocked off the block. Noise from the nearby waterfall may have been a factor. (*Source: Bradley Roach.*)

ANOTHER TAKAKKAW FALLS INCIDENT: *On September 27, at approximately 12:30 a.m., Banff dispatch received a call from a concerned camper reporting headlamps on the cliffs to the left of Takakkaw Falls. Two rescuers responded and climbed three pitches to reach the stranded party, who were 30 meters apart, at around 3:50 a.m. The party had attempted to rappel with a single rope from a station that only works for a 60-meter rappel. (Even though they had two ropes, they rigged the rappel with a single rope out of fear of getting their ropes stuck.) The climbers had misread the guidebook description of which rappel anchors to use with a single rope, and they lacked the skills—route-finding, rope ascension—to get themselves out of their predicament.*

LOWERING ERROR | Rope Too Short, Inattention
Alberta, Banff National Park, Lake Louise

June 18 was a busy day at the Back of the Lake. We were a group of seven; everyone knew each other, but not everyone had climbed together. Everyone was a physically strong climber, which may have led to a sense of complacency.

Several of the climbers decided to link Public Enemy into Bloodsport (5.11-) after seeing another party do the same. The other party said the combined pitches totaled 43 meters, but their 80-meter rope "did the trick" for lowering, with stretch. Person 1, one of our group members, said his rope was 80 meters. Person 1 linked the two pitches and attempted to lower to the ground. Person 2, lowering Person 1 with his Grigri, was looking up at Person 1 when the rope pulled through the belay device. There was no knot, and the rope was not 80 meters. It was 70 meters.

Person 1 fell about five meters to a ledge, bounced off his butt with his back to the cliff, and then ricocheted between a tree trunk and the cliff. When he hit the ground he had fallen 12 meters. Person 1 was evacuated with the help of many climbers and Banff Visitor Safety. He had a concussion and minor scrapes to his head where he had collided with the tree. He had not been wearing a helmet.

ANALYSIS

There were a lot of assumptions made that day, including the obvious one that the rope was long enough for this route. Then came the negligence of not tying a stopper knot on a long route and not wearing a helmet. Contributing factors included the busyness at the crag and rotating partners who had not climbed together before. Assumptions of experience were made based on physical abilities. It was a casual day of climbing, and the casual attitude led to a grave error. (*Source: Anonymous member of the group.*)

ROCKFALL | Off-Route, Crowds
Alberta, Mt. Temple, East Ridge

Two rockfall incidents on the popular east rige of Temple resulted in injuries and evacuations. On July 30, a party of three high on the route had just made the long traverse left across loose ledges to gain gullies through the Black Towers. Route-finding can be difficult in this area, and this party began ascending the wrong gully. After one pitch, the leader realized he was off route and started to rappel back down. He dislodged a large rock that struck the head of one of the other climbers, cracking the helmet and causing a concussion. The team was able to retreat back across the ledge to a high point on the ridge, from which they were evacuated.

On August 9 there were multiple parties lined up on the east ridge. In the middle of the route is the Big Step, a steep, three-pitch section of 5.7 climbing. A climber in a lower group was struck by rock dislodged by a climber above, sustaining a shoulder injury. The climber was lowered to a large ledge below the Big Step with the assistance of the upper party and evacuated from this ledge.

ANALYSIS

The risk of rockfall or dropped gear is always present when climbing or belaying below others. Clear communication between parties, anticipating the trajectory of possible rockfall, establishing protected belay stances, and timing the ascent of each pitch can minimize the risk. Crowding sometimes can be mitigated by earlier starts, as well as efficient leads and change-overs at belay stances, spreading parties out. Congestion on popular routes will continue to be a challenge with the growing popularity of climbing. Sometimes it's best to choose a less crowded route or wait for a quieter day.

ROCKFALL
Alberta, Mt. Lefroy, Fuhrmann Ledges

On July 16, a guided party of three was ascending the Fuhrmann Ledges route to Abbot Pass Hut. They had to make an exposed traverse under a large gully near the base of the northwest face of Mt. Lefroy in order to access the ledge that crosses the face. The group agreed on a plan to jump to the right (away from the gully) if anyone shouted "rock!" during this traverse. Approximately five minutes into their traverse, a large rock fell toward the party. One member of the group jumped to the right but was still struck in the right arm, sustaining a fractured humerus. The group descended to a sheltered area from which they were evacuated.

ANALYSIS
Exposure to rockfall cannot be avoided on the Fuhrmann Ledges route. However, the risk can be minimized by proper planning and rapid passage through the most exposed areas. If the party had not discussed the plan to jump right prior to their traverse, this incident might have resulted in more serious injuries.

RAPPEL ERROR | Burned Hands
Alberta, Banff National Park, Mt. St. Bride

On August 23, two climbers were attempting the southeast ridge of Mt. St. Bride, near Lake Louise. To gain the base of the route, climbers must do a 45-meter overhanging rappel. The first climber successfully rappelled and moved off to the side to perform a fireman's belay. The second climber came down partway, then stopped to remove his gloves because, he said, they were not working for him. As he was nearing the ground, he lost control and started to slide too quickly. His partner on the ground attempted to stop him by pulling the ropes tight, but one rope was hooked on scree so he was able to pull only one strand. This slowed the falling climber, preventing serious injury, but not enough to prevent rope burns to the rappeller's hands. The climbers were using 8.5mm half ropes, and the injured climber had a first-generation Petzl Reverso device and a prusik as a backup. However, the accessory cord was new and the prusik did not catch.

The climbers bandaged the wound and contemplated their options: try to climb back out to their bivy or descend to the east and undertake a long bushwhack back to camp (at least 20 kilometers or 12.5 miles). Neither option seemed reasonable, given the state of the injured climber's hands, so they called for a rescue.

ANALYSIS
Wearing gloves while rappelling will prevent rope burns but also may promote rapid rappels, which itself increases risk. A slow, steady rappel is always preferable. Thinner ropes afford less friction in rappel devices; check the device's recommended rope diameter range and comply with manufacturer guidelines. The weight of the rappeller (and pack weight) may be a factor as well.

A prusik backup or other third-hand rappel backup requires greater care with thin ropes. It should be tested in a safe setting before a full rappel. The accessory cord used should be supple and at least 2mm thinner than the climbing rope.

FOUR STRANDED PARTIES | Underestimated Difficulties
Alberta, Banff National Park, Mt. Rundle Traverse

There were four separate rescues of uninjured but stranded groups of climbers on the Rundle Traverse in the summer of 2017. This 18-kilometer (11-mile) traverse follows a ridge across the many summits of Mt. Rundle. The terrain is mostly scrambling, which increases in difficulty from east to west in both route-finding and technical climbing (low fifth class). It is usually done in one very long day.

All of the rescues were in the more technical sections of the ridge, which can require some roped climbing as well as rappels, depending on experience and comfort level. Some of the parties had lengths of rope and a small rack, and some did not. All of the parties called for help by cell phone later in the day and were evacuated via helicopter long line, either that evening or at dawn the next day.

ANALYSIS
All of these groups said the route was much harder and longer than they expected. People often go light to traverse Rundle and may not bring as much gear as they might carry normally. The difficulties are encountered past the halfway mark along the traverse, so the ease of a "forward retreat" could be a factor in decision making: Climbers elect to keep going rather than turn around and risk being benighted. (All parties should carry enough gear for an unexpected night out.) Limestone is notoriously tricky for route-finding if climbers are not accustomed to that type of terrain, and online descriptions often are inadequate. These parties had cell phones and were able to initiate a rescue. However, from other nearby areas cell phones may not work, and emergency satellite devices would be required to call for assistance.

RAPPEL ANCHOR FAILURE
Alberta, Little Sister

On July 22 a party reached the summit of Little Sister via the Grassi Route (northeast buttress) late in the day and chose to descend the way they'd come up because they were familiar with the terrain. During their descent, the climbers set up a rappel from a rock horn. After inspecting the slings in place around the horn, the first climber rappelled to the next anchor. The second climber had begun her rappel when the horn collapsed and she tumbled down the slope. She sustained injuries to her head and torso, but the party was able to descend to a large ledge where they spent the night. They called for a rescue the next morning.

ANALYSIS
The dislodging of natural rock anchors such as horns, chockstones, and boulders is among the most common causes of rappel anchor failure. It is easy to be lulled into complacency by an established anchor, but each anchor must be inspected thoroughly every time. (One way is to pound or kick the rock and observe vibration, movement, or dirt and gravel displacement.) When in doubt, find another anchor or leave a backup. In this case, the common practice of placing a piece to back up the anchor for the first person down would not have prevented this accident, because the horn held in place for the first rappeller but not the second.

TABLES

TABLE I: REPORTED CLIMBING ACCIDENTS

Year	Number of Accidents Reported		Total Persons Involved		Injured		Fatalities	
	USA	CAN	USA	CAN	USA	CAN	USA	CAN
1951	15	n/a	22	n/a	11	n/a	3	n/a
1952	31	n/a	35	n/a	17	n/a	13	n/a
1953	24	n/a	27	n/a	12	n/a	12	n/a
1954	31	n/a	41	n/a	31	n/a	8	n/a
1955	34	n/a	39	n/a	28	n/a	6	n/a
1956	46	n/a	72	n/a	54	n/a	13	n/a
1957	45	n/a	53	n/a	28	n/a	18	n/a
1958	32	n/a	39	n/a	23	n/a	11	n/a
1959	42	2	56	2	31	0	19	2
1960	47	4	64	12	37	8	19	4
1961	49	9	61	14	45	10	14	4
1962	71	1	90	1	64	0	19	1
1963	68	11	79	12	47	10	19	2
1964	53	11	65	16	44	10	14	3
1965	72	0	90	0	59	0	21	0
1966	67	7	80	9	52	6	16	3
1967	74	10	110	14	63	7	33	5
1968	70	13	87	19	43	12	27	5
1969	94	11	125	17	66	9	29	2
1970	129	11	174	11	88	5	15	5
1971	110	17	138	29	76	11	31	7
1972	141	29	184	42	98	17	49	13
1973	108	6	131	6	85	4	36	2
1974	96	7	177	50	75	1	26	5
1975	78	7	158	22	66	8	19	2
1976	137	16	303	31	210	9	53	6
1977	121	30	277	49	106	21	32	11
1978	118	17	221	19	85	6	42	10
1979	100	36	137	54	83	17	40	19
1980	191	29	295	85	124	26	33	8
1981	97	43	223	119	80	39	39	6
1982	140	48	305	126	120	43	24	14
1983	187	29	442	76	169	26	37	7
1984	182	26	459	63	174	15	26	6
1985	195	27	403	62	190	22	17	3

Year	Number of Accidents Reported		Total Persons Involved		Injured		Fatalities	
	USA	CAN	USA	CAN	USA	CAN	USA	CAN
1986	203	31	406	80	182	25	37	14
1987	192	25	377	79	140	23	32	9
1988	156	18	288	44	155	18	24	4
1989	141	18	272	36	124	11	17	9
1990	136	25	245	50	125	24	24	4
1991	169	20	302	66	147	11	18	6
1992	175	17	351	45	144	11	43	6
1993	132	27	274	50	121	17	21	1
1994	158	25	335	58	131	25	27	5
1995	168	24	353	50	134	18	37	7
1996	139	28	261	59	100	16	31	6
1997	158	35	323	87	148	24	31	13
1998	138	24	281	55	138	18	20	1
1999	123	29	248	69	91	20	17	10
2000	150	23	301	36	121	23	24	7
2001	150	22	276	47	138	14	16	2
2002	139	27	295	29	105	23	34	6
2003	118	29	231	32	105	22	18	6
2004	160	35	311	30	140	16	35	14
2005	111	19	176	41	85	14	34	7
2006	109	n/a	227	n/a	89	n/a	21	n/a
2007	113	n/a	211	n/a	95	n/a	15	n/a
2008	112	n/a	203	n/a	96	n/a	19	n/a
2009	126	n/a	240	n/a	112	n/a	23	n/a
2010	185	n/a	389	n/a	151	n/a	34	n/a
2011	157	n/a	348	n/a	109	n/a	29	n/a
2012	140	15	309	36	121	12	30	2
2013	143	11	283	24	100	5	21	4
2014	112	10	170	19	89	8	28	1
2015	173	20	258	52	111	16	37	4
2016	175	23	302	58	134	17	32	6
2017	162	24	n/a	n/a	116	19	34	2
TOTAL:	7,818	1,061	14,108	2,192	6,481	792	1,696	311

TABLE II: ACCIDENTS BY LOCATION

Geographical Districts	1951–2016 Number of Accidents	Deaths	2017 Number of Accidents	Deaths	Injuries
Canada*					
Alberta	568	148	11	1	11
British Columbia	341	130	9	1	7
Yukon Territory	40	28	3	0	1
New Brunswick	1	0	0	0	0
Ontario	40	9	0	0	0
Québec	32	10	1	0	0
East Arctic	8	2	0	0	0
West Arctic	2	2	0	0	0
United States					
Alaska	621	223	14	1	14
Arizona, Nevada, Texas	131	26	2	0	2
Atlantic–North	1193	161	28	2	20
Atlantic–South	238	44	11	0	11
California	1559	334	36	8	25
Central	143	18	1	0	1
Colorado	978	246	28	12	17
Montana, Idaho, South Dakota	102	41	1	0	1
Oregon	269	130	5	1	4
Utah, New Mex.	230	74	13	1	10
Washington	2050	344	11	5	6
Wyoming	644	157	12	4	5

*Canada figures include no data from 2006–2011; new data is included from 2012–2016

TABLE III: ACCIDENTS BY CAUSE

	1951–2016 USA	*1959–2016 CAN.	2017 USA	2017 CAN.
Terrain				
Rock	5358	578	117	16
Snow	2686	375	37	7
Ice	311	23	7	1
River	25	3	0	0
Unknown	25	11	1	0

	1951–2016 USA	*1959–2016 CAN.	2017 USA	2017 CAN.
Ascent or Descent				
Ascent	4295	631	63	8
Descent	1413	402	59	11
Unknown	308	15	34	3
Other[1]	40	2	6	2
Immediate Cause				
Fall or slip on rock	4173	316	58	4
Fall on snow or ice	1194	221	21	2
Falling rock, ice, or object	703	148	8	5
Exceeding abilities / Inexperience	604	36	1	0
Illness[2]	465	27	4	1
Stranded / Lost	418	63	10	3
Avalanche	334	133	1	4
Rappel Failure / Error[3]	414	55	15	3
Lowering Error[7]	6	1	11	1
Exposure	287	14	0	0
Loss of control / Glissade	243	18	3	0
Nut / cam pulled out	295	11	2	0
Failure to follow route	259	36	0	0
Fall into crevasse / moat	190	52	7	0
Faulty use of crampons	127	7	0	0
Piton / ice screw pulled out	95	13	0	0
Ascending too fast	79	0	1	0
Skiing[4]	73	14	8	2
Lightning	68	7	0	0
Equipment failure	18	3	0	0
Other[5]	631	39	3	3
Unknown	73	10	13	2
Contributory Causes				
Climbing unroped	1110	174	6	0
Exceeding abilities / Inexperience	1057	206	15	2
Placed no / inadequate protection	929	105	8	3
Inadequate equipment / clothing	769	74	9	3
Weather	542	76	4	1
Climbing alone	470	74	3	0
No helmet	390	75	5	1
Inadequate belay[6]	303	29	7	1
Nut / cam pulled out	244	33	13	0

	1951–2016 USA	*1959–2016 CAN.	2017 USA	2017 CAN.
Poor position	253	28	5	4
Darkness	185	23	2	0
Party separated	139	12	3	0
Loose rock / failure to test holds	131	47	7	4
Piton / ice screw pulled out	87	15	0	0
Failed to follow directions / route	98	18	16	1
Exposure	68	16	0	0
Illness[2]	41	9	2	0
Equipment failure	22	7	1	0
Other[5]	325	102	1	1
Age of Individuals				
Under 15	1249	12	0	0
15-20	1352	204	7	0
21-25	1604	259	33	3
26-30	1539	215	31	0
31-35	2165	18	15	0
36-50	3547	145	24	1
Over 50	436	37	18	0
Unknown	2322	585	26	24
Sex[7]				
Male	252	36	131	16
Female	85	7	33	5
Not known	66	5	9	7
Experience Level				
None/Little	1940	308	10	0
Moderate (1 to 3 years)	1825	359	7	3
Experienced	2529	488	46	14
Unknown	2682	606	84	11
Month				
January	278	26	2	2
February	250	60	10	2
March	398	74	7	1
April	498	42	4	2
May	1049	68	9	2
June	1291	79	26	2
July	2128	270	22	3

August	1203	203	28	5
September	2085	79	9	3
October	531	42	10	2
November	256	24	5	0
December	135	27	4	0
Unknown	51	3	4	0
Type of Injury/Illness (Data since 1984)				
Fracture	1721	251	42	4
Laceration	863	84	18	0
Abrasion	429	79	9	1
Bruise	607	89	2	0
Sprain / strain	496	38	2	0
Concussion	355	31	15	3
Hypothermia	183	19	2	0
Frostbite	157	13	4	0
Dislocation	175	16	7	0
Puncture	58	14	0	0
Acute Mountain Sickness	53	0	1	0
HAPE	93	1	1	0
HACE	37	0	1	1
Other[8]	457	57	8	5
None	394	202	10	3

N.B. Data change: The 1986 and 1997 editions had some repeat data from previous years. The corrections are reflected in the cumulative data.

[1] Some accidents happen when climbers are at the top or bottom of a route. They may be belaying or setting up a rappel, for example. This category was created in 2001. The category "unknown" is primarily because of solo climbers.

[2] These illnesses/injuries, which led directly or indirectly to an accident, included HAPE and HACE.

[3] These included inadequate anchors, uneven ropes, no knots in rope ends, simul-rappelling errors, pendulum swings, and attaching device incorrectly. Prior years' data may have included lowering errors.

[4] This category covers ski mountaineering. Backcountry ski touring or snowshoeing incidents, including those involving avalanches, are not counted in these tables.

[5] These included failure to self-arrest, dropped rope, cornice collapse, anchor failure, belayer pulled into wall, intoxication, and earthquake.

[6] These included miscommunication, ineffective belay, and no belay.

[7] Category introduced in 2016. Lowering errors included rope too short, miscommunication, and lowering with wrong rope.

[8] These included rope burns, snow blindness, appendicitis, various knee injuries, partial amputation, degloving, pneumothorax, knocked-out teeth, and other unspecified injuries.

Note: Injuries are counted only once in each category for a given incident. For example, an accident that results in three broken bones will only be listed once under "Fracture."

MOUNTAIN
RESCUE
ASSOCIATION

✛ Saving lives through rescue and mountain safety education

✛ Accrediting rescue teams in mountain rescue disciplines

✛ 100 rescue teams / 2,000 professional volunteer mountain rescuers

✛ MRA teams perform 5,000 search & rescue operations in the U.S. each year

✛ Member teams do not charge for their services

Go to www.mra.org to learn more and find backcountry safety information.

Photo: © Howard Paul

Courage. Commitment. Compassion.
www.mra.org